BEAD CROCHET
JEWELRY

BEAD CROCHET JEWELRY

An Inspired Journey Through 27 Designs

BERT RACHEL FREED and
DANA ELIZABETH FREED

PHOTOGRAPHS BY GEORGE ROSS

ST. MARTIN'S GRIFFIN ☀ NEW YORK

BEAD CROCHET JEWELRY. Copyright © 2012 by
Bert Rachel Freed and Dana Elizabeth Freed. Photographs
copyright © 2012 by George Ross Photography.
All rights reserved. Printed in China.
For information, address St. Martin's Press, 175 Fifth Avenue,
New York, N.Y. 10010.

www.stmartins.com

ISBN 978-0-312-67294-2

Design by Gretchen Achilles/Wavetrap Design

First Edition: July 2012

10   9   8   7   6   5   4   3   2   1

This book is dedicated to Larry B.,
who showed us that everyone has something to create,
and that all those who make something by hand
can do a job "well done."

CONTENTS

INTRODUCTION

BEADING IS A JOURNEY

When we took our first seed bead weaving class in 1999, we had no idea that we were embarking on a unique journey. How could we know that one class could leave us with such a desire to learn everything there is to know about beading? We never expected to feel so propelled by inspiration from our teacher, our classmates, and each other. Over the next several years, through numerous courses and independent exploration, we developed such a passion for beadwork that in 2006, we began our own company *The Well Done Experience*, devoted to perpetuating the craft; a line of couture jewelry, *Chicken and the Egg Designs*, followed in 2008. Through our "travels" around the world of beading we formed and fostered treasured relationships with others. We learned that, by creating together, we helped each other overcome obstacles at our darkest times and celebrate our proudest moments.

The adventures of beadwork began long before we discovered its magic. Beads have existed as a means of communication since the dawn of recorded time. People have used beads as currency in trade and as a mode of indicating status and familial ties. From the Native Americans to the ancient Egyptians to the earliest African tribes, beads have been used to document people's histories and memories, both personal and collective. On a smaller scale, the same has been true for us. We have traded ideas and designs, joy and sorrow, between each other and countless others—all via the delicate web of beadwork.

It is with these ideas in mind that we constructed this book. The designs and accompanying instructions are all original, but we have asked our friends and students to use each set of directions as a starting point for their own creativity. Here, we share with you some of the ways in which they made the pieces their own. We encourage you to do the same. Learn the techniques, use our patterns; but never forget that you, too, are on a journey to create pieces that are entirely your own.

Like you, we are still searching for new discoveries. We hope to fill a lifetime with a limitless search for new ways to use beads. Whether you are just embarking on your bead voyage or have been on the road for years, we hope that what we share with you will enhance your beading adventure

Bert and Dana

MATERIALS
AND
TOOLS

A comprehensive list of the materials and tools that we recommend

for the projects in this book and beyond.

THREAD

GENERAL TIPS

Usually, we encourage you to use the thickest possible thread that the hole in your beads will allow. Following this rule will make your work more flexible and secure. When you use thread that is too thin for your bead size, you will find that your piece will be very stiff and uncomfortable to wear.

Most importantly, don't use cotton or silk! We know that many artists believe in using "pure" materials, and we respect the fundamentals behind this ideal; however, the fact remains that cotton and silk will disintegrate. We hope that our work will outlive us by centuries!

Luckily, there are many options in the nylon and polyester families, and new products are being introduced to the market regularly.

NYLON AND POLYESTER

THE C-LON THREAD FAMILY
C-Lon is an excellent product because it comes in several thicknesses, the small spools make it easy to transport, and the color selection is vast. The materials list for each project will refer to the C-Lon thread you should use, but in this section you will find appropriate substitutes. We encourage you to experiment with the other threads we recommend as well, and use the ones with which you are most comfortable.

C-LON BEAD CORD This is the perfect weight for most bead crochet projects. It comes in 86-yard spools and is currently available in 104 colors (though new colors are being introduced regularly). This thread can be used for most seed beads size 8/0 or larger (we'll get to bead sizes soon).

C-LON BEAD CORD SUBSTITUTES
Beadsmith Nylon #18 (previously known as Mastex): Available in 165-yard spools and 11 colors.

Conso Nylon #18: Available in 165-yard spools and 14 colors.

CONSO NYLON #18

BEADSMITH NYLON #18

C-LON BEAD CORD

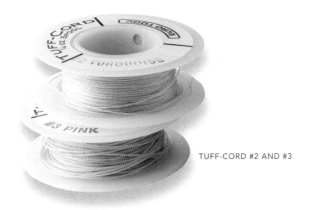

TUFF-CORD #2 AND #3

C-LON MICRO CORD When you are ready to crochet with size 11/0 seed beads (which are tiny), small pearls, semiprecious and even precious stones, use this very fine thread. Because the thread is so thin, we recommend using it only when hole size makes it necessary. It is very strong, but because it does not have very much body it does not behave properly with larger beads that have small holes. C-Lon Micro comes in 320-yard spools and is currently available in 32 colors (and counting).

C-LON FINE WEIGHT BEAD CORD When using seed beads size 8/0 or smaller beads with smaller (more stubborn) holes—such as certain drops and daggers—and some semiprecious stones, you may need to use this thinner thread. It comes in 136-yard spools and is currently available in 16 colors (with new colors being introduced regularly).

C-LON MICRO CORD

C-LON FINE WEIGHT SUBSTITUTES

Tuff-Cord #2: Available in 66-yard spools and 16 colors.

Tuff-Cord #3 (slightly thicker than #2): Available in 49-yard spools and 16 colors.

C-LON FINE WEIGHT BEAD CORD

C-LON FINE WEIGHT SUBSTITUTE

Tuff-Cord #1: Available in 98-yard spools and 16 colors.

TUFF CORD #1

YARN, METALLIC THREAD, LEATHER, AND MORE

Though we almost exclusively use one of the previous threads, we are always looking for new alternatives that will allow us to expand the potential of our beadwork. We encourage you to try new materials as well. There are several factors to keep in mind when trying out alternative threads. First, whatever thread you use must be strong. Try ripping it with your hands; if it comes apart easily, then it's definitely not the right thread to use. If it doesn't rip at first, try wetting it and see if it frays or stretches. Next, remember that you have to string the beads you want to use onto your thread, so the thread must be thin enough for you to do so. For example, you won't be able to string 11/0 seed beads onto a C-Lon Bead Cord–weight thread. Finally, for certain projects, your thread will be touching your skin. Be sure that the texture of the thread will not be uncomfortable against your neck or wrist.

FIRELINE

FIRELINE 8 LB. BRAIDED
BEAD THREAD

You may need to use FireLine to reinforce your closure when you use focal beads. Although you will never use this thread to crochet, it is an important material for every bead crocheter to have in stock. Available in three colors—Crystal (which is basically white), Smoke (charcoal gray), and Flame Green—it comes in 125-yard, 300-yard, and 1,500-yard spools. We recommend Smoke if you plan on purchasing only one color; it disappears into your work better than Crystal. However, you can use a Sharpie to change the color of Crystal to match your beads, which is a great option.

ASSORTED ALTERNATIVE THREADS

STEEL CROCHET HOOKS

The steel hooks used for bead crochet are very small and sized by number. As the number of the hook goes up, the hook gets smaller (e.g., a size 8 hook is actually smaller than a size 4 hook). It is important to use the appropriate hook size for your thread. Because everyone's tension is different, we recommend trying several sizes before deciding which one is right for you. If you find that your work is too loose, use a hook one or two sizes smaller than recommended; conversely, if your work is too tight, move to a slightly larger hook. Larger hooks that are used for regular crocheting are sized by letter, with an A being the smallest.

Generally speaking, when using C-Lon Bead Cord (or a comparable thread), use anywhere from a size 3 to 5 hook; most people are comfortable with a size 4. When using C-Lon Fine Weight (or a comparable thread), use a size 7 or 8 hook. When using C-Lon Micro, use a size 10 or 11 hook. When using an alternative thread, try several different hook sizes until the tension of the piece feels right.

In general, the head of your hook needs to be large enough to grab the thread but small enough that your stitches are snug. After you become comfortable with bead crochet, you will instinctively know the right size hook for the thread you are using.

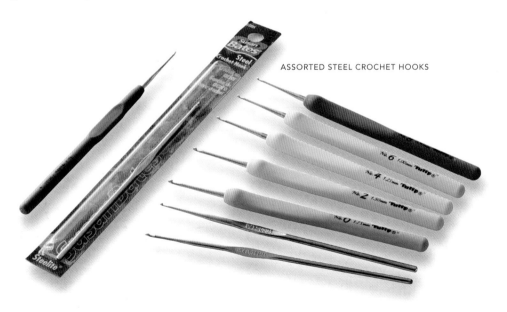

ASSORTED STEEL CROCHET HOOKS

BEADS

Almost anything you can imagine is available in bead form. Resin? Yes. Paper? Yes. Diamonds? Yes—you can even buy diamond beads! We would love to tell you about all the beads available in the world, but then we would never get to the projects. As always, we encourage you to try as many different shapes and sizes as possible, because there are no rules!

Remember that not all beads are created equal; two beads of the "same size" made by two manufacturers might be very different. Beads that are coated, lined, or dyed may lose color or peel over time and with wear. We recommend *against* using bi-cones (like Swarovski crystals), because their edges and holes are sharp and they can cut your thread. Be sure to check the holes and edges of your beads before you begin a project.

We encourage you to combine materials—just because you have chosen to work with pressed-glass beads doesn't mean you can't also use semiprecious stones in the same project. Let color and texture combinations guide you, not conventional ideas of what is "precious" and what is "less valuable." To get you started, here is a brief description of the beads we like best for bead crochet.

GLASS

SEED BEADS

Seed beads (tiny glass beads) come in many sizes, but the most commonly used for bead crochet are 6/0, 8/0, and 11/0. As the size of the bead goes up, the number goes down, so a size 6/0 is actually larger than an 8/0. (The system refers to the approximate number of beads per inch when laid flat. In other words, there are approximately six 6/0 seed beads per inch.)

11/0 SEED BEADS

8/0 SEED BEADS

6/0 SEED BEADS

CZECH SEED BEADS

JAPENESE SEED BEADS

PRESSED-GLASS ROUNDS

Pressed-glass round beads are virtually the same as fire-polished crystals, without the facets. They come in the same sizes (3mm, 4mm, etc.) and thus can be used for any project that requires fire-polished crystals, and vice versa. They are less expensive, but they are also less brilliant. Like fire-polished crystals, they come in hundreds of colors and finishes.

Look at the quality and shape of seed beads before you make a selection; most Japanese seed beads are consistent, while many Czech and Chinese seed beads vary in size—even if they are from the same lot. If you find beads that are misshapen, too small, or too large, discard them. They are the least expensive beads you can use, so it is worth it to cull the rejects to ensure that your finished product is uniform.

FIRE-POLISHED CRYSTALS

Fire-polished crystals are a relatively inexpensive way to make your work spectacular, because their faceted cut catches the light and creates sparkle. They come in hundreds of colors and finishes, including matte, AB, Marea, and Vitral. For bead crochet we usually prefer size 3mm, 4mm, and 6mm, but occasionally we also go smaller (2mm) and larger (8mm and higher).

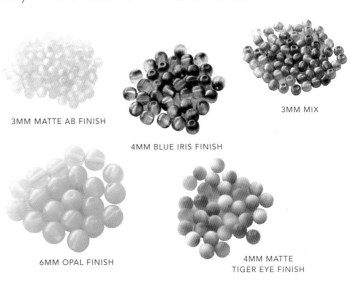

3MM MATTE AB FINISH

4MM BLUE IRIS FINISH

3MM MIX

6MM OPAL FINISH

4MM MATTE
TIGER EYE FINISH

6MM MATTE AB FINISH

4MM OPAL FINISH

4MM MAREA FINISH

6MM VITRAL FINISH

3MM AB FINISH

6MM METALLIC FINISH

3MM TWO-TONE FINISH

4MM LUSTER FINISH

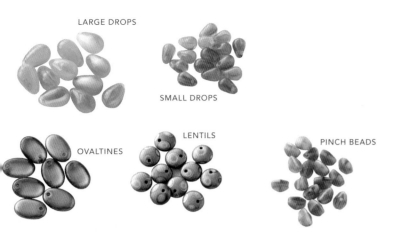

LARGE DROPS

SMALL DROPS

OVALTINES

LENTILS

PINCH BEADS

GEMSTONE DONUTS

These beads (also sometimes referred to as crystal rondelles) sit beautifully when crocheted because of their shape, which is larger around the middle than in height. They are available in many sizes, including 2×3, 3×5, 4×7, and larger. While the sizes listed are ideal for crocheting, the larger sizes (6×9, 7×11, etc.) make excellent focal beads.

PRESSED-GLASS SHAPES

Daggers, drops, leaves, lentils, squarelettes, ovaltines, coin beads, pinch beads, and other shapes add texture and interest when used alone or combined with seed beads, crystals or rounds. We like these shapes because they are side-drilled, so when they are crocheted into your piece, most of the bead "sticks out" and is visible. Other interesting shapes can be used as well, to different effect. Try them all!

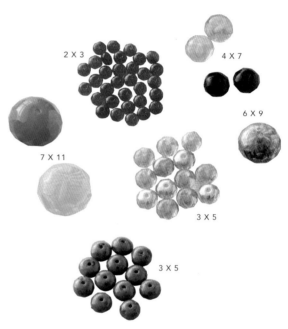

2 X 3

4 X 7

6 X 9

7 X 11

3 X 5

3 X 5

COIN BEADS

LARGE LEAVES

SMALL LEAVES

SQUARELETTES

LARGE DAGGERS

SMALL DAGGERS

FAUX PEARLS

REAL PEARLS

PEARLS (FAUX AND REAL)

While diamonds may be a girl's best friend, pearls are as "classic" as the "little black dress." Always dependable and beautiful, they are perfect for every occasion. There are benefits and drawbacks to using both real and faux pearls in bead crochet. Faux pearls are wonderful because their holes are large enough to facilitate stringing on heavier threads like C-Lon Bead Cord or C-Lon Fine Weight. They are also perfectly even. Believe it or not, they can also be more expensive. The only faux pearls we recommend are those by Swarovski, because, unlike other faux pearls, their coating does not peel off.

Real pearls have the obvious advantage of being natural. They come in every shape, size, and, thanks to irradiation, color. Their holes are smaller (more appropriate for C-Lon Fine Weight or C-Lon Micro), making them more difficult to string.

PRECIOUS AND SEMIPRECIOUS STONES

The biggest problem with using stones is that their holes are small and sharp, especially those of faceted stones. When buying these beads, make sure that the holes will be large enough for the thread you want to use (remember that you always want to use the thickest thread possible). Also, look at the quality of the stones. The less expensive ones tend to have irregular holes, which make them more difficult to string. They are also usually duller in color and have less brilliant faceting. Higher-quality stones, though more expensive, will look better and have larger, more even holes. Stones can be substituted for crystals or pressed glass for the projects in this book, as long as the sizes are consistent (e.g., you can use a 4mm round semiprecious bead instead of a 4mm fire-polished crystal). Note that if you make a substitution, you may have to change your thread as well.

ASSORTED PRECIOUS AND SEMIPRECIOUS STONES

ASSORTED COPPER, SILVER, AND
GOLD-FILLED BEADS

FOCAL BEADS

When we refer to focal beads, we mean large accent beads that are used in small quantity (sometimes only one) to enhance a piece. They are not made from any specific material, so they can be glass, metal, semiprecious stone, etc. The most important trait of a focal bead is a hole large enough for your thread to go through several times when you reinforce the connection.

METAL BEADS

Metal beads (such as sterling silver, gold-filled, copper, etc.) are measured in millimeters, so they can be used for any project in this book that calls for a bead of the same size. When buying metal beads, be sure they are seamless; many have seams that can open up while you work with them or after the piece has been finished. Also make sure that the beads are not plated. For example, you can buy a base-metal bead that is plated with sterling silver. This does not mean that the bead is made of sterling silver; it means that a poor-quality metal has been coated with sterling silver. Over time, the plating will wear away and you will be left with uneven, unattractive beads in your piece.

ASSORTED FOCAL BEADS

OTHER SUPPLIES

GENERAL BEADING SUPPLIES

You need a pair of sharp scissors with a fine point, and a tape measure, as well as a practical work surface such as a bead mat. Using a bead mat will prevent your beads from rolling away.

PLIERS

You need needle-nose pliers, round-nose pliers, and wire cutters if using standard jewelry findings.

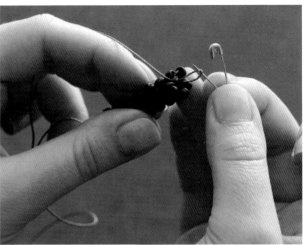

NEEDLES

Everyone finds his or her own favorite way to string beads onto thread. You can use a big-eye needle, a small darning or sewing needle, a size 10 beading needle (for thinner threads), a flex needle, or even a blue GUM EEZ-thru floss threader. Try different methods until you find what's right for you in each situation. Often, it's easier to just load your beads directly onto the thread and bypass the needle completely.

SAFETY PINS

Safety pins are often your best friends when bead crocheting. Whenever you walk away from your work, whether for a bathroom break or a weeklong break, you will want to hold the working loop of your project with a safety pin. Just insert the open safety pin into the loop and close the pin. This will prevent your work from unraveling.

Safety pins are also helpful if you drop a stitch; you can pick up the working loop much more easily with the point of the pin than you can with your hook.

Lastly, safety pins are useful for marking your place if you need to count rows or to measure.

ASSORTED FINDINGS AND BUTTONS

FINDINGS AND BUTTONS

Depending on the project, you might need to incorporate standard jewelry findings. These include headpins, earring posts or hooks, pin backs, chains, and clasps. We do not recommend magnetic clasps, because they can open easily and you can lose your jewelry. When choosing findings, decide what color your want your metal to be and whether you prefer better-quality materials (silver, copper, etc.) or less-expensive materials (base metal). When buying jump rings, make sure they are soldered (fused shut). If not, they can open and your piece can break.

Buttons are an interesting way to enhance your work. They can be used as closures and as focal elements. Try ending a bracelet with a striking button and wearing it in the front as the focal piece.

GETTING STARTED

Take a trip through the basic methods and some useful hints

that will help you learn and master bead crochet.

A NOTE ON THE ORGANIZATION OF THIS BOOK

After years of working with students, we found that achieving success with circular crochet is more likely if you start with a chain stitch project. We know that you may be eager to get to the advanced projects, but we strongly recommend making at least one project from each section before moving on to the next. Each section provides you with the foundations you need to move up to the next level. We like to think of bead crochet as math: you have to know how to add, subtract, multiply, and divide before you can learn algebra. Or (if our math analogy frightens you), you need to know the alphabet before you can start spelling words!

This section contains general information to help you troubleshoot as you are getting started. At the beginning of each project section, you will find detailed instructions for the techniques needed for the projects in that section. In the last section, Advanced Tips and Tricks, you will find additional suggestions for making your bead crochet experience as smooth as possible.

GENERAL INFORMATION

WORKING WITH THREAD

In bead crochet you always begin by stringing on all the beads for your project (or the piece of the final project that is worked separately) directly onto the spool of thread. Once you have strung your beads, *do not* cut the thread from the spool. You will crochet all the beads and then cut the thread when the piece is complete.

QUANTITIES

It is difficult to give exact quantities for each project, because we all crochet with different tension, and have different wrist and neck sizes and tastes. Each set of instructions gives you the approximate quantities for the project. You may need to adjust your quantities by using fewer or more beads, so that you can achieve the look and fit that best suits you.

STRINGING

If your beads are stubborn and you can't use a needle to string them, cut the end of your thread at an angle, creating a point. If the thread begins to fray or lose stiffness, trim it as often as necessary. You can also use a dab of base-coat nail polish to stiffen the end.

STRETCH

Bead crochet pieces will inevitably stretch over time, even when you use nylon thread. Because bangles are pushed over your hand with every wearing, you may find that these especially may become too large. We recommend that after you finish crocheting each rope, but before you begin the finishing process, stretch out your piece by pulling firmly. Begin in the middle and work your way out toward the ends. Make bracelets slightly shorter than the desired length. They may be a little difficult to put on the first few times you wear them, but eventually they will stretch out to the correct size. You will find that pieces made with larger beads will stretch more than pieces made with smaller beads, so be sure to take that into account when selecting beads and measuring your work.

TENSION

Tension refers to the tightness of your stitches when you crochet, and everyone's tension is different. Your tension affects the final size and look of your piece. Looser tension yields a larger piece and shows more thread; if your tension is very loose, your beads will not sit correctly. Conversely, tighter tension creates a smaller piece with less visible thread. If your tension is very tight, your piece will be stiff and inflexible. Your goal should be to have a flexible piece with even tension and beads that sit correctly. Try different hook sizes until this is achieved and you find your comfort zone.

BASIC STITCHES AND TECHNIQUES

As with any craft, there are important fundamental skills that are important to know in order to learn bead crochet. You need to be comfortable holding the hook and thread, and know how to make a chain stitch and a slip stitch. If you have never crocheted before, we recommend practicing with a worsted-weight yarn and a size F or G crochet hook. Then practice with C-Lon Bead Cord and a size 4 steel crochet hook without beads, so that you become comfortable with these materials before beginning your first project.

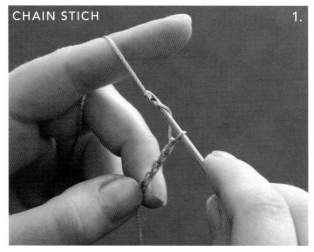

CHAIN STICH 1.

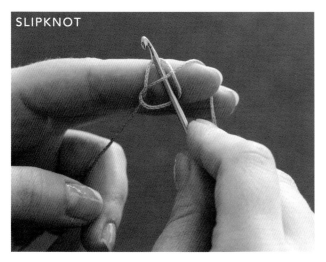

SLIPKNOT

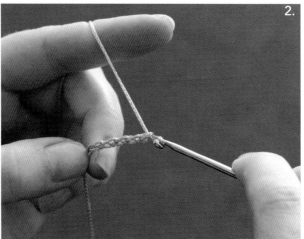

2.

SLIPKNOT

All crochet projects begin with this simple knot. Make a loop by crossing the tail of the thread over itself. Then cross the tail behind the loop. Reach into the loop and grab the tail. Pull it up through the loop (not all the way), creating a new loop. You should have at least an 8-inch tail. Tighten and adjust your loop to fit comfortably around your hook.

CHAIN STITCH

1. Use your hook to draw a loop through the existing loop on the hook (you will have only one loop on your hook at all times). Repeat until the chain is the desired length.

2. Be sure to keep your chain stitches consistent. If your stitches are too tight or too loose, your work will look messy.

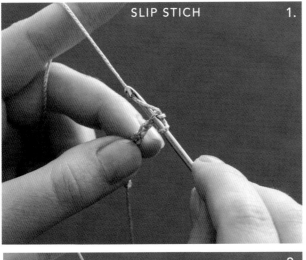

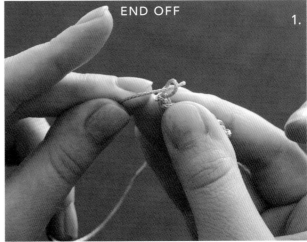

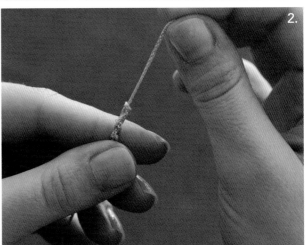

SLIP STITCH

1. Start with a chain stitch base. Insert your hook into the second stitch from the hook. You now have the original loop on your hook as well as the loop from the stitch below (two loops on hook).

2. Yarn over (wrap the working yarn around your hook) and pull through both loops on the hook. You will have only one loop on your hook now. Repeat across the row.

END OFF

1. Cut your thread, leaving an 8-inch tail.

2. Pull the tail through the loop tightly until it makes a knot.

BURYING YOUR THREAD TAILS IN CIRCULAR CROCHET PIECES

1. Using a tapestry needle, sew directly into the piece away from the direction of your invisible join, focal bead, or clasp, coming out about ¼ inch from where you inserted your needle. If you have trouble pulling the thread through, this is probably a sign that you have split a thread, so take your needle out and try again.

2. Weave in and out of the piece in this manner, being careful not to sew through any beads. Sewing through a bead can warp its position or cause it to break. Make sure that your stitches are close together. If your stitches are too far apart it is likely that your thread will cross over a bead and be visible. If you are using focal beads, it is a good idea to sew your tails in one direction and then back in the other direction. You do not need to make any knots; they are lumpy and unnecessary. (For specifics of burying thread using different finishing techniques, see "Finishing Circular Crochet Projects" on pages 47–51.)

CHAIN STITCH PROJECTS

Chain stitch with beads is a relatively simple technique that looks complicated. Thread color is an important design element because it is so visible—the thread color you choose will greatly affect the final look of your piece. In this section, you will learn the technique from start to finish.

BASIC TECHNIQUES

HOW TO CHAIN STITCH WITH BEADS

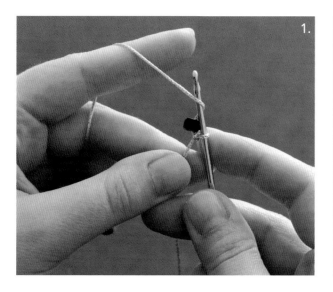

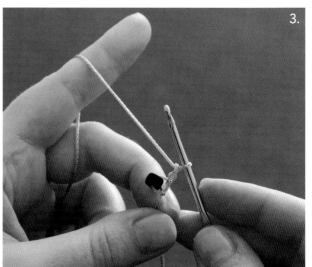

1. String all of your beads onto the spool and do not cut the thread. Make a slipknot, leaving an 8-inch tail. Insert crochet hook into slipknot. Push down one bead all the way against your slipknot.

2. Make one chain stitch, capturing the first bead in the loop to secure it in place.

3. You will have one loop on your hook. Next make a second chain stitch without a bead. Continue to repeat these two steps.

Making an empty chain stitch in between the stitches with beads allows for a more flexible chain. Unless otherwise specified, all our projects require one empty chain stitch between each bead.

HOW TO FINISH CHAIN STITCH PROJECTS

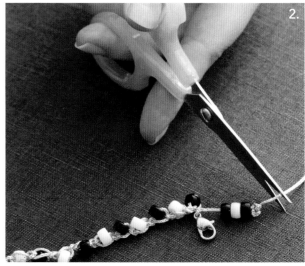

FINISHING WITH A KNOT

1. You will have two tails, one on each end of
your piece. Tie the tails together with two or three
knots tightly against the beads. Add a few decorative
beads onto one tail, pushing them close to the top
and securing them with two overhand knots. Repeat
with the other tail. Snip the excess thread, leaving
approximately ¼ inch, and let the two ends dangle.

NOTE: The tails can be symmetrical or different. You
can use many beads on each tail, for an interesting
design element, or just one on each so that they are
barely noticeable.

FINISHING WITH A CLASP

2. Thread one tail through one side of your clasp.
Tie several knots to secure. Add a few decorative
beads onto the end of the tail and secure with
overhand knots. Snip the excess thread and let the
end dangle. Repeat with the second tail.

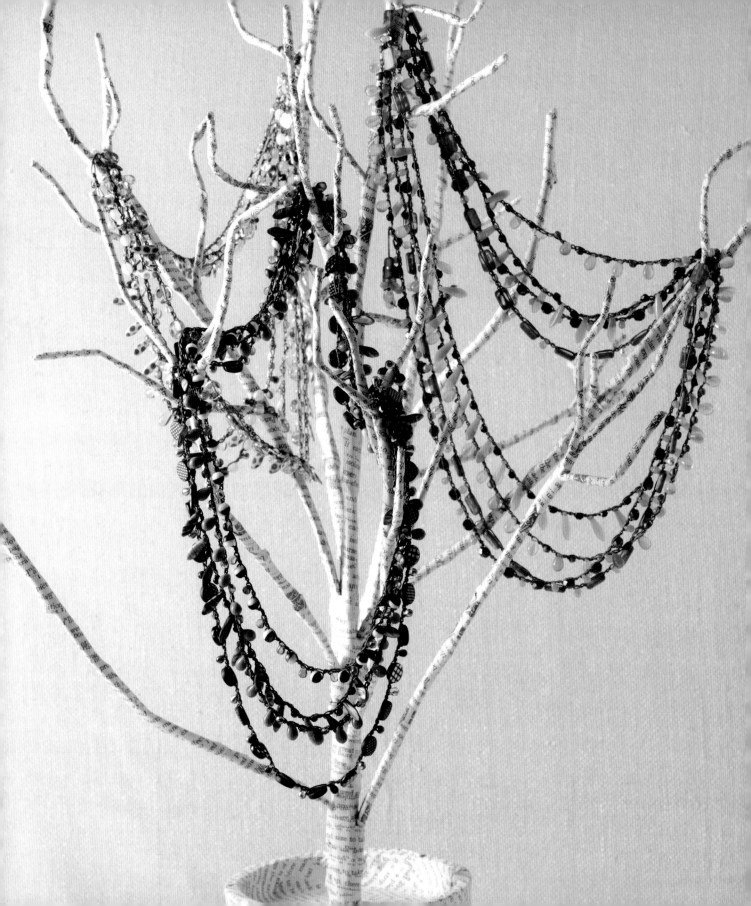

BANG-FOR-YOUR-BUCK NECKLACE

DESIGNED BY BERT AND DANA

Although this project is simple enough for the novice bead crocheter, the fabulous final product will have everyone convinced you're an expert. Using four different bead patterns in a single piece, you can create a dramatic necklace that can be wrapped two to four times around your neck for various looks. When wrapped four times, the necklace appears to be four separate strands. Even if you are a master bead crocheter, you will definitely want to add this simple yet versatile piece to your collection.

WHAT YOU NEED

- 50 small drops in color A
- 49 6mm fire-polished crystals
- 38 small drops in color B
- 37 glass coin beads
- 56 4mm crystals in color C
- 55 large daggers
- 50 4mm crystals in color D
- 49 extra-large drops
- C-Lon Bead Cord

MAKE IT!

PATTERN 1: String 1 small drop in color A. Then string *[1 6mm crystal, 1 small drop in color A]; repeat from * until all of those beads have been strung.

PATTERN 2: String 1 small drop in color B. Then string *[1 coin bead, 1 small drop in color B]; repeat from * until all of those beads have been strung.

PATTERN 3: String 1 4mm crystal in color C. Then string *[1 dagger, 1 4mm crystal in color C]; repeat from * until all of those beads have been strung.

PATTERN 4: String 1 4mm crystal in color D. Then string *[1 extra-large drop, 1 4mm crystal in color D]; repeat from * until all of those beads have been strung.

Make a slipknot, leaving an 8-inch tail. Insert crochet hook. Chain one stitch with a bead, one stitch without a bead. Repeat until you have crocheted all your beads.

End off the thread. Finish following "Finishing with a Knot" (page 29).

NEXT TIME . . .

Try using other shapes like lentils, squarelettes, ovaltines, and rondelles. Almost any beads can be used for this project!

STRAND-TOGETHER NECKLACE

DESIGNED BY BERT AND DANA

In this necklace, four separate patterned strands using semiprecious chips in combination with simple seed beads create an interesting juxtaposition between the organic and the polished. The four strands come together with focal beads that provide a simple way of finishing the piece, but also add drama and weight. Using a neutral-colored thread will emphasize the "natural" elements in your piece, whereas using a bright-colored thread will make it more playful and eclectic.

WHAT YOU NEED

- 44 semiprecious chips each in four colors: A, B, C, and D
  or
- 88 semiprecious chips each in two colors: A and B
- 180 size 6/0 seed beads
- Several focal beads
- C-Lon Bead Cord (or Fine Weight if the semiprecious bead holes are small)

MAKE IT!

If using four colors of semiprecious beads: Decide which is color A, which is B, which is C, and which is D.

STRAND 1: String 1 A. Then string *[1 seed bead, 1 A]; repeat from * until you have strung all the A beads.

Make a slipknot, leaving an 8-inch tail. Chain one stitch with a bead, one stitch without a bead. Repeat until you have crocheted all your beads. End off the thread leaving an 8-inch tail, and set this strand aside.

STRAND 2: String 1 B. Then string *[1 seed bead, 1 B]; repeat from * until you have strung all the B beads.

Work as for strand 1.

STRAND 3: String 1 C. Then string *[1 seed bead, 1 C]; repeat from * until you have strung all the C beads.

Work as for strand 1.

STRAND 4: String 1 D. Then string *[1 seed bead, 1 D]; repeat from * until you have strung all the D beads.

Work as for strand 1.

If using two colors: Decide which is A and which is B.

STRAND 1: String 1 A. Then string *[1 seed bead, 1 A]; repeat from * until you have strung half of the A beads (44 beads).

Make a slipknot, leaving an 8-inch tail. Chain one stitch with a bead, one stitch without a bead. Repeat until you have crocheted all your beads. End off the thread leaving an 8-inch tail, and set this strand aside.

STRAND 2: String 1 B. Then string *[1 6/0 seed bead, 1 B]; repeat from * until you have strung half of the B beads (44 beads).

Make a slipknot, leaving an 8-inch tail. Chain one stitch with a bead, one stitch without a bead. Repeat until you have crocheted all your beads. End off the thread leaving an 8-inch tail, and set this strand aside.

STRANDS 3 AND 4 (make two): String 1 A. Then string *[1 seed bead, 1 B, 1 seed bead, 1 A]; repeat from * until you have strung half of the remaining A beads (22 beads).

Make a slipknot, leaving an 8-inch tail. Chain one stitch with a bead, one stitch without a bead. Repeat until you have crocheted all your beads. End off the thread leaving an 8-inch tail, and set this strand aside.

FINISHING: Make sure that the four strands are all approximately the same length. If not, pull out or add a few beads as necessary.

Hold the four ending tails and the four beginning tails together in one hand. Tie the eight tails together in a secure overhand knot. Slip the large glass focal bead onto all eight strands and push it all the way up to the knot. (If the hole on this bead is large enough, it may even cover the knot completely.) String on small, medium, and small focal beads. Tie an overhand knot at the base to secure them and snip off the excess, leaving ¼ inch of thread. If you are unable to string these three focal beads on all eight threads, string on as many as the holes will allow and snip the remaining threads as close to the base of the large focal bead as possible.

NEXT TIME . . .
Try stringing your chips in different patterns, using more than one color chip in each strand. For example, string the first strand in an AB pattern, the second strand in a CD pattern, and the third and fourth strands using all four colors in different ratios.

◎◎ BEAD CROCHET REDUX ◎◎

As in all aspects of our lives, our first instinct is not always the best one. It doesn't matter how long you work on a piece; if your end result isn't pleasing to you, don't settle. We always encourage our students to rip out some of their work while they are learning a technique so they can become comfortable with the process of reworking their piece until they decide it's perfect.

Meaghan brought a magazine advertisement to class one week, and wanted to use it as inspiration for designing her next piece. While she was choosing her colors (matching them carefully to those in the image), she decided that she didn't like some of the tones and would omit them. The following week she returned to show us her creation (a lariat), but she was displeased. Her disappointment led to an important realization: in this case, it wasn't the individual colors that were appealing about the ad, but it was the way they looked in combination with one another that was so visually pleasing.

She remade the lariat, adding the colors she had originally left out, and tweaking some of her patterning. The revised version of the lariat was similar in some ways, but so much better! Don't ever be afraid to tear something out and start again; in bead crochet, just as in life, it is essential to learn from your mistakes.

VICTORIAN NOSTALGIA NECKLACE

DESIGNED BY BERT AND DANA

This necklace was designed to celebrate the delicacy of the Victorian era, while updating an antique element through a modern interpretation. You can use any object as the pendant, not just a locket or a charm. Try using something unconventional, like a coin, a game piece, or another found object.

WHAT YOU NEED

- 24 7mm–9mm rice or coin pearls
- 24 5mm–6mm cornflake pearls
- 202 3mm semiprecious stones
- C-Lon Fine Weight
- Antique pendant or locket
- Toggle (optional)

MAKE IT!

STRAND 1: String *[1 cornflake pearl, 1 rice or coin pearl, 1 cornflake pearl, 3 semiprecious stones]; repeat from * 19 more times.

Make a slipknot, leaving an 8-inch tail. Chain one stitch with a bead, one stitch without a bead. Repeat until you have crocheted all your beads. End off the thread leaving an 8-inch tail, and set this strand aside.

STRAND 2: String *[3 semiprecious stones, 1 rice or coin Pearl, 3 semiprecious stones]; repeat from * 21 more times.

Make a slipknot, leaving an 8-inch tail. *[Chain one stitch with a bead, one stitch without. Repeat 3 more times. Next, chain all three semiprecious stones together into a cluster, chain one stitch without a bead]; repeat from *, alternating the semiprecious stones crocheted individually and those crocheted in a cluster.

FINISHING WITHOUT A TOGGLE CLASP: Make sure that the two strands are approximately the same length. If not, pull out or add a few beads as necessary.

Hold all four tails together and tie an overhand knot. Thread two tails through the pendant and tie all four tails together with a double knot. On one tail, string on 3 semiprecious stones and 1 rice or coin pearl, and secure this dangle with a knot. Repeat once more. On the third tail, string on 2 semiprecious stones and 1 cornflake pearl, and secure this dangle with a knot. Repeat once more. Trim your tails to ¼ inch.

FINISHING WITH A TOGGLE CLASP: Using your two ending tails, tie a double knot around the bail (loop) of the toggle bar. On one ending tail, string on 3 semiprecious stones and 1 rice or coin pearl, and secure dangle with a knot. On the other tail, string on 2 semiprecious stones and 1 cornflake pearl, secure with a knot. Trim tails to ¼ inch. Using your two beginning tails, tie two knots around the bail (loop) of the pendant and the bail of the toggle ring. Finish the two beginning tails the same way as the ending tails.

NEXT TIME:

Use a coordinating monochromatic color scheme.

DANGLE-A-GEM EARRINGS

DESIGNED BY BERT AND DANA

Because the nature of the chain stitch method is light and airy, it was difficult to design earrings that would have enough weight to dangle properly. The addition of the focal beads to the bottom of each strand helped solve this challenge. These earrings are a wonderful gift because they are quick and easy to make. With the right bead choice, they can also look very impressive.

WHAT YOU NEED

- 36 3mm round or fire-polished beads
- 8 2 × 3 gemstone donuts
- 4 8mm fire-polished beads or large gemstone donuts
- Earring wires or posts
- C-Lon Fine Weight

MAKE IT!

EARRING (make two): String 10 3mm beads, the earring finding, 8 3mm beads. Note that there is a front and a back to the earring; you need to string the earring finding on upside down (with the back facing you).

Make a slipknot, leaving an 8-inch tail. Start by crocheting an empty chain, then chain one stitch with a bead and one without a bead. Crochet the earring finding (tightly) as though it were a bead. When you have crocheted all the beads, crochet an empty chain and end off your thread, leaving an 8-inch tail. Hold the earring finding in one hand and pull down on the two crocheted strands with the other. This will make everything sit in place properly.

On one tail, string 1 2 × 3 gemstone donut, 1 8mm bead, 1 2 × 3 gemstone donut. Tie an overhand knot just below these three beads to hold them in place and trim your tail, leaving ¼ inch. Repeat with the other tail.

NEXT TIME . . .

Experiment with different earring lengths by adding more or fewer beads on each side.

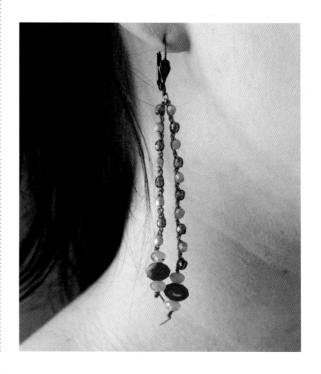

39

CIRCULAR CROCHET PROJECTS

In this section, you will learn the basics of circular crochet. Each of these projects is finished with focal beads or a clasp. Until you become proficient in making bead crochet ropes from start to finish, it is much easier to finish projects using beads or clasps.

HOW TO CIRCULAR CROCHET WITH BEADS (FOUR AROUND)

We suggest you practice by making a sample using four large, different-colored beads and thicker thread—such as pony beads on worsted-weight yarn with a size G crochet hook—before moving on to the first project in this section.

- 20 red pony beads
- 20 dark blue pony beads
- 20 yellow pony beads
- 20 turquoise pony beads
- Cotton worsted-weight yarn
- Size G crochet hook

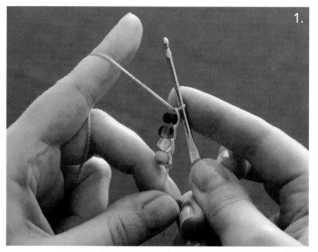

MAKE IT!
String *[1 red bead, 1 dark blue bead, 1 yellow bead, 1 turquoise bead]; repeat from * until you have strung all your beads.

1.   Make a slipknot, leaving an 8-inch tail. Insert crochet hook

Chain four stitches with beads (one stitch with a turquoise bead, one with a yellow bead, one with a dark blue bead, and one with a red bead). The tail will be pointing down, or toward the bottom of the crochet hook.

2.   Reposition the tail so that it is pointing away from you (toward the top of the hook) and make sure the beads are facing up.

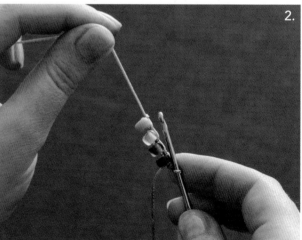

Insert the hook into the first chain (closest to the tail), under the turquoise bead, into the thread loop (two loops on hook). This forms a circle.

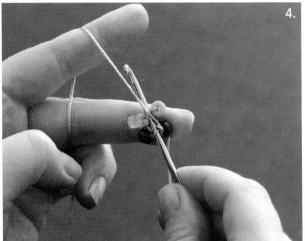

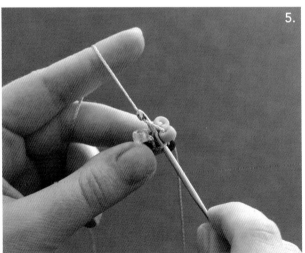

3. Push the turquoise bead so that it is sitting to the right of the hook, with the hole of the bead facing up. If the bead is not pushed to the right of the hook, the stitch will be incorrect.

4. Bring the thread that is attached to the spool (not the tail) up between the red bead and the turquoise bead. Bring the thread across the top of the thread loop that is on the hook. If your thread gets caught under the turquoise bead, your stitch will not come out correctly.

5. Push down a new turquoise bead so that it is sitting on top of the turquoise bead from the row below. The new bead should also be to the right of the hook. Pull the thread through the two loops on the hook, making sure that you have caught the new turquoise bead in the stitch.

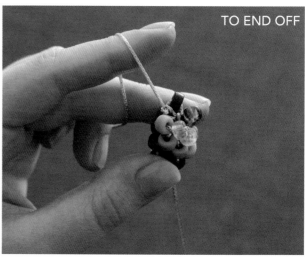

6. Insert your hook into the thread loop with the yellow bead. (Notice that you are working counterclockwise.)

Push the yellow bead so that it is sitting to the right of the hook, with the hole of the bead facing up.

Bring the thread up between the turquoise bead and the yellow bead. Bring the thread across the top of the thread loop that is on the hook. Make sure it is on top of the yellow bead, not underneath.

Push down a new yellow bead so that it is sitting on top of the yellow bead from the row below. Make a slip stitch, ensuring that you have caught the new yellow bead in the stitch.

Insert your hook into the thread loop with the dark blue bead.

Push the dark blue bead so that it is sitting to the right of the hook, with the hole of the bead facing up.

Bring the thread up between the yellow bead and the dark blue bead. Bring the thread across the top of the thread loop that is on the hook. Make sure it is on top of the dark blue bead, not underneath.

Push down a new dark blue bead so that it is sitting on top of the dark blue bead from the row below. Make a slip stitch, ensuring that you have caught the new dark blue bead in the stitch.

Insert your hook into the thread loop with the red bead.

Push the red bead so that it is sitting to the right of the hook, with the hole of the bead facing up.

Bring the thread up between the dark blue bead

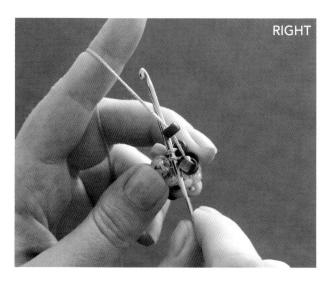

RIGHT

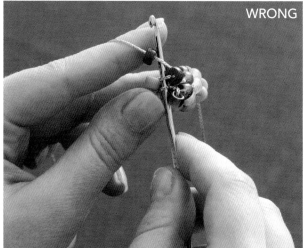

WRONG

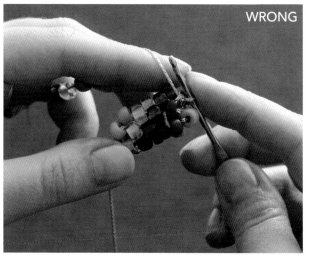

WRONG

and the red bead. Bring the thread across the top of the thread loop that is on the hook. Make sure it is on top of the red bead, not underneath.

Push down a new red bead so that it is sitting on top of the red bead from the row below. Make a slip stitch, ensuring that you have caught the new red bead in the stitch. You have just completed the second row.

Repeat from the beginning until you have crocheted all your beads.

To end off, cut your thread from the spool, leaving an 8-inch tail. Thread the tail through the loop and pull, securing a knot.

RIGHT: The most common mistake people make is orienting the thread incorrectly. If you have pushed your bead all the way to the right, the thread should comfortably cross right over the loop and the hook.

WRONG: If not, the thread can get caught under the bead.

You will know you have made a mistake because a bead sticks out of your work. If you have made a mistake, pull out your work until the mistake is removed and continue working as normal.

The first three rows are the hardest. At the end of each row, make sure you can locate the four beads you worked in the last round—these four beads are worked in the next round. If you are having trouble starting, just continue working even if you make mistakes. You can practice beginning again once you are more comfortable with working on the subsequent rows.

You will notice after you have completed a few rows correctly that the beads in the last row you crocheted sit differently. The beads in all other rows sit with their holes facing up; however, the beads in the last row you crocheted sit with their holes facing to the side. When you insert your hook into a stitch and push the bead to the right, it makes that bead lie in the correct position. Knowing this will help you identify which stitch to go into when adding a new bead.

We have found that using a little mantra will help you remember the steps when you are learning. You may need to create your own, but we suggest something like the following:

1. Insert hook.

2. Push the bead to the right.

3. Bring thread over (on top).

4. Bring down a new bead and pull thread through.

Verbally and physically repeating the steps help the motions become muscle memory, so that eventually you won't even realize that your hands know the correct method.

If you want to work your rope more than four beads around, simply chain the corresponding number of beads in the foundation row (e.g., for a bracelet six around, chain six stitches in the foundation row and work six stitches in every following row).

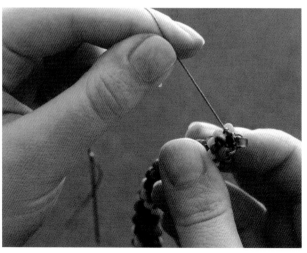

THE YELLOW BEAD IS THE NEXT STITCH YOU WOULD CROCHET, SO IT IS THE FIRST BEAD YOU SEW INTO

PULLING THE THREAD THROUGH PUTS THE BEAD INTO POSITION

When you have finished crocheting your rope, you need to know how to finish it properly. (Also see: "Burying Your Thread Tails in Circular Crochet Pieces" on page 25.)

For all the following techniques, you first need to complete STEP 1.

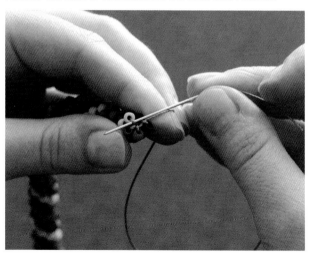

AFTER YOU HAVE COMPLETED THE ROW, SEW BACK INTO THE FIRST BEAD ONCE MORE

STEP 1

Cut thread from the spool leaving an 8-inch tail, and pull the tail through the loop to make a knot. Then, thread the tail onto a tapestry needle and locate your last bead (it will be the highest bead right next to the knot). Insert the needle into the same stitch you would crochet next (the bead counterclockwise to the last bead).

Make sure the bead is to the right of the needle (the way it is when you crochet), and pull the needle all the way through.

This puts the bead in the right position. Insert your needle into the next counterclockwise stitch

and pull the needle through as you did for the first stitch. Continue in this manner until you have worked all the way around the beads in the last row, ensuring that you go back into the first stitch again to complete the round.

Then complete as follows (see pages 48–49).

OPEN END WITHOUT FOCAL BEADS (LARIAT)

After completing STEP 1, bury your threads in your work. See "Burying Your Thread tails in Circular Crochet Pieces" on page 25.

OPEN END WITH FOCAL BEADS (LARIAT)

1. After completing STEP 1, string your focal bead(s) onto your tail. It may be necessary to bypass the needle altogether, in which case, thread your bead(s) directly onto the string. The last bead you put on should be a small seed bead or crystal. Go back through the other bead(s) from the opposite direction, skipping the last little bead. This will act as a stopper.

2. Pull your thread as tightly as possible and sew back into your rope. If possible, repeat several times so that you have really reinforced your ending bead(s). Bury your tails. (You may also need/want to reinforce with FireLine; see page 50.)

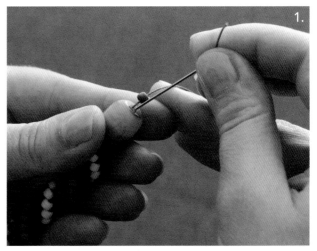

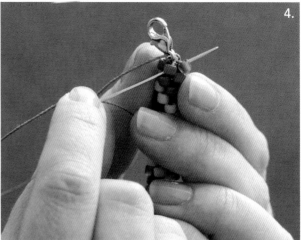

OPEN END WITH A CLASP OR BUTTON
(NECKLACES AND BRACELETS)

3.   After completing STEP 1, insert your thread into the bail (loop) of one side of your clasp and into the top of your rope on the side opposite the tail's origin.

4.   Repeat several times to reinforce and bury your threads. Repeat with the other side of the clasp.

   If using a button, attach the shank of the button as you would the bail of a clasp. On the other side, string on several small beads to create a loop to fit the button (you will need to use a little trial and error). Sew into the rope and reinforce the loop several times. Bury your thread.

CONTINUOUS WITH FOCAL BEADS
(NECKLACE OR BRACELET)

5.   Complete STEP 1. Insert the ending tail through the bead from one direction and the starting thread through the bead from the other direction, so that the two threads crisscross through the center of the bead.

6.   Thread a darning needle onto one thread and sew into the rope, coming out about ¼ inch down, being careful not to sew through a bead.

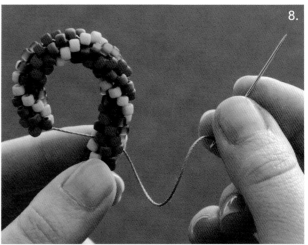

7. Repeat with the other tail. Pull the threads away from each other very tightly—the focal bead will eventually put stress on the join, causing the thread to stretch a little. The more tightly you pull when joining, the less you will see the thread when it eventually stretches.

Bury your tails in opposite directions. If the piece is a bracelet, make sure you sew your tails *at least* halfway around, so that the two tails meet in the middle, directly opposite the focal beads. We recommend burying your tails all the way around. If you are finishing a necklace, sew your tails at least 4 to 6 inches into the piece. The deeper you bury your tails, the more secure your piece will be.

TOGGLE LOOP (NECKLACE OR BRACELET)
There is no exact science to this process, so as always, let your intuition guide you. Making your seam invisible can be achieved as long as the end lies flat against the rope.

8. Complete STEP 1. Fold your piece, creating a loop of the appropriate length (large enough for your toggle to fit through but small enough so that

it won't slip out). Sew into the rope, coming out straight across.

9. Turn your needle around, and sew directly back across the rope and into the end.

Repeat several times. Make sure you sew into and come out of the end from different directions, so that the end of the rope gets tacked down all the way around.

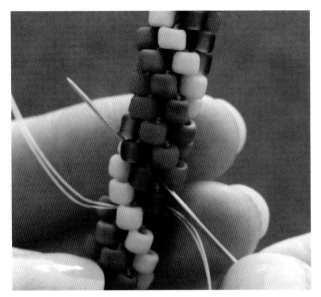

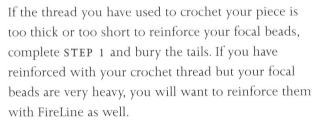

ADD THE FIRELINE BY SEWING IT IN STARTING FOUR TO SIX INCHES
BELOW THE END OF THE ROPE BEFORE YOU BEGIN TO REINFORCE THE
FOCAL BEAD

If the thread you have used to crochet your piece is too thick or too short to reinforce your focal beads, complete **STEP** 1 and bury the tails. If you have reinforced with your crochet thread but your focal beads are very heavy, you will want to reinforce them with FireLine as well.

Thread FireLine 8 lb. Test thread onto a small needle, like a size 10 beading needle or a small sewing needle. Begin sewing the FireLine into the piece several inches above the end, approximately 4 to 6 inches into the piece. Leave a short tail sticking out. Using the same method as Burying Your Tails (see page 25), sew the FireLine into the piece toward the ending. Reinforce the focal beads by sewing back and forth through them several times as you would sew through them using crochet thread.

If you are reinforcing a lariat, finish by burying the FireLine back into your work, up toward where you began sewing in the FireLine.

If you are reinforcing a continuous necklace or bracelet, bury your FireLine in the opposite direction, on the other side of the necklace or bracelet.

Snip your FireLine tails as close to the work as possible.

CENTER OF THE UNIVERSE BRACELET

DESIGNED BY BERT AND DANA

Spirals may look complicated, but they are actually the simplest way to learn circular bead crochet. By slightly varying the bead sizes in this bracelet, we created subtle texture while still working with the basic spiral pattern. We love the design of this bracelet because it reminds us that, although our paths may be long and winding, we always return to the center of our own universe.

WHAT YOU NEED

- 58–65 6mm fire-polished crystals in color A
- 58–65 4mm fire-polished crystals in color B
- 58–65 6/0 seed beads in color C
- 58–65 6/0 seed beads in color D
- (**NOTE:** You will need an equal amount of A, B, C, and D. Your quantities will vary depending on your wrist size and choice of focal beads.)
- 2 small focal beads
- 1 large center focal bead
- C-Lon Bead Cord

MAKE IT!

String *[1A, 1B, 1C, 1D]; repeat from * until you have strung all your beads.

Before beginning to crochet, line up your three focal beads and measure the length.

Work in circular crochet four beads around until the bracelet is the focal bead–length shorter than the desired length. (For example, if your three focal beads total 1 inch in length, and you want your bracelet to be 8 inches when complete, crochet until you have 7 inches of beaded rope.) End off your thread.

String your focal beads (one small, then the large, and one small) onto one tail and finish using the method for Continous Finishing with Focal Beads. (page 49)

NEXT TIME . . .

Substitute the focal bead join with an interesting button or beautiful toggle.

TIERED BRACELET

DESIGNED BY BERT AND DANA

Once you have mastered the spiral, you may not yet feel confident enough to begin working in a single color. This bracelet allows you to keep track of your work in a different way. In a spiral you are always putting color A on top of color A, B on top of B, etc. Here you will work four beads of color A in a single round, so in the following round you will be working color B on top of color A four times. You can keep track of the beads in each round by counting four beads of a single color. If you crochet a B on top of a B, you'll know that you've decreased a stitch.

WHAT YOU NEED
- 56 2 × 3 gemstone donuts in color A
- 56 2 × 3 gemstone donuts in color B
- 56 3 × 5 gemstone donuts in color C
- 44 4 × 7 gemstone donuts in color D
- Large focal bead(s)
- C-Lon Bead Cord

MAKE IT!
String *[4 A, 4 B, 4 C, 4 D, 4 C, 4 B, 4 A]; repeat from * 10 more times.
Before beginning to crochet, line up your three focal beads and measure the length.

Work in circular crochet four beads around until the bracelet is the focal bead–length shorter than the desired length. (For example, if your three focal beads total 1 inch in length, and you want your bracelet to be 8 inches when complete, crochet until you have 7 inches of beaded rope.) End off your thread.
String your focal beads (one small, then the large,

and one small) onto one tail and finish using the method for Continous Finishing with Focal Beads. (page 49).

NEXT TIME . . .

Use different shapes for each tier. For example, use lentils, squarelettes, ovaltines, and 4mm fire-polished crystals.

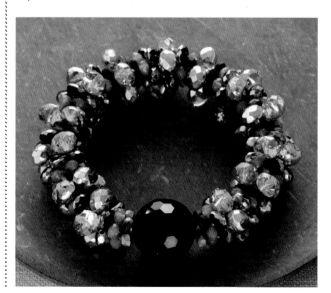

54

SOUP-ER VERSATILE NECKLACE AND LARIAT

DESIGNED BY BERT AND DANA

Double, double, toil and trouble! Creating a "witches' brew" of assorted beads can be the most fun you have beading. Follow our simple soup "recipe" for creating the perfect mix, or try your own! You can buy premade mixes as well, but we really enjoy watching the potion evolve as we add more ingredients. Make more than you think you need—it's better to have some left over than to run out. You will find that it's very difficult to replicate a soup accurately unless you know the exact quantities of each bead used.

The sky is the limit with these versatile pieces, so we encourage you to be creative and do some of your own designing. Remember, there is no "right" or "wrong" answer.

WHAT YOU NEED

- 3–4 tubes size 8/0 or 6/0 seed bead "bead soup" (or a mix that combines the two sizes)
- Coordinating focal beads (as many as you want)
- C-Lon Bead Cord or C-Lon Fine Weight, depending on the size of your beads

NOTE: See The Science of Soup (page 59)

MAKE IT!

String all your beads. You can work four, five, or six around, depending on whether you want your rope thin or chunky. If you are making a long necklace (long enough to wrap at least once), we recommend that you crochet four around. If you are making a shorter necklace or a lariat, you can work thicker.

Crochet until desired length.

Finish using Open End (page 48) with Focal Beads for an open lariat, or Continous Finishing with Focal Beads (page 48) for a closed necklace.

NEXT TIME . . .

Use the leftover soup to make some matching bangles!

◎◎ THE SCIENCE OF SOUP ◎◎

The following are some suggestions to help you get mixing your "soups." Some people like their ingredients pureed, while others like them in large chunks. The same is true for beads: Some people prefer mixes with subtle variations, while others like those with many different elements.

We made one of our favorite bead soups of all time by adding a capful of size 8/0 seed beads in every color we owned. The result was a lush kaleidoscope of color that coordinated with every item in our wardrobes.

Generally, the more colors you use, the more interesting your piece will look. It is possible to make a soup using just two colors, but you will find that if there is a lot of contrast your piece may look splotchy. If you combine two similar colors, your piece can look subtly shaded or appear to be an interesting solid.

If you mix shapes or sizes that are too varied, you may find that your finished product looks lumpy or does not behave properly. We encourage you to experiment with combining different shapes and sizes, but those that are not too dramatically different (e.g., do not use a size 11/0 seed bead in a soup with 8mm fire-polished crystals). A good rule of thumb is to mix shapes and sizes that would normally use the same size thread.

There is no perfect recipe for bead soup, but the suggestions that follow will help you get started. Remember to add new colors or shapes in small quantities first, then add more until you like the ratio. Mix your beads in a large bowl or container so that you don't have to worry about beads falling all over your table or floor.

1. Color variegation: Choose a color and combine different shades and finishes of that color using the same size beads. If you choose blue, for example, use at least four or five shades ranging from sky to navy in shiny, matte, translucent, etc.

2. Bead type: Choose a type of bead and a particular finish (e.g., matte 4mm crystals or lined 6/0 seed beads) and mix many colors of that kind.

3. Single color: Choose a color and mix several different shapes and sizes in that one color. This is particularly dramatic in solid black or white.

4. Color scheme: Be inspired by one of your favorite fabrics or paintings, and use those colors in your soup. Be sure to note the ratio of colors; if there is only a dash of yellow in the piece that has inspired you, use only a dash of yellow in your soup.

ROPE-AND-CHAIN NECKLACE

DESIGNED BY BERT AND DANA

Our family has a fascination with all things nautical. Many of us incorporate ships, anchors, and nautical flags into our home decor, though we don't often have the opportunity to travel by water. The two of us recently noticed that the utilitarian ropes and chains used on boats are also quite beautiful. We were inspired by the way these objects look in combination with one another and designed this necklace.

WHAT YOU NEED

- 10 tubes 6/0 seed beads in main color (MC)
- (Less than) 1 tube 6/0 seed beads in color B
- (Less than) 1 tube 6/0 seed beads in color C
- 126 2 × 3 gemstone donuts (GD)
- 108 daggers
- 18 8mm fire-polished crystals
- C-Lon Bead Cord
- Clasp

MAKE IT!

CHAIN STITCH STRAND 1: String 2 MC, 3 B, 2 MC. Then string *[1 C, 1 GD, 1 dagger, 1 GD, 1 C, 2 MC, 3 B, 2 MC]; repeat from * 25 more times.

Make a slipknot, leaving an 8-inch tail. Crochet *every* stitch with a bead, until you have crocheted all your beads. (Note: Do not crochet an empty chain in between chains with beads.) End off, leaving an 8-inch tail.

CHAIN STITCH STRAND 2: String 3 MC. Then string *[1 C, 1 dagger, 1 C, 1 GD, 1 dagger, 1 GD, 1 crystal, 1 GD, 1 dagger, 1 GD, 1 C, 1 dagger, 1 C, 3 MC]; repeat from * 17 more times.

Crochet as for strand 1.

ROPE: String on all but 20 remaining MC. (The remaining beads will be used for the closure.)

Make a slipknot, leaving an 8-inch tail.

Work in circular crochet four around until you have crocheted all your beads. Before ending off, make sure that your rope is approximately the same length as your chain stitch strands. If it is much longer or shorter, add or remove beads as necessary.

ASSEMBLY: Attach the clasp to the rope (see Open End with Clasp (page 48) and bury the tails. Attach strands 1 and 2 to the same clasp. Add 5 MC to each dangle.

NEXT TIME . . .

Make a shorter necklace. This one has a chain stitch strand 1 nine repeats long, a chain stitch strand 2 six repeats long, and a rope 18 inches long.

LEAVES AND DAGGERS AND DROPS, OH MY!

I. LARIAT

DESIGNED BY BERT

One of the most exciting aspects of bead crochet is the possibility for texture and movement. I like my pieces to look organic—as though they have grown from nature, but without using "natural" shapes like flowers and leaves. We have made countless variations of this lariat, experimenting with length, proportion, and different bead shapes.

My lariats are usually muted in tone and matte in texture; Dana's tend to be brighter and blingier.

WHAT YOU NEED
- 1,200 4mm fire-polished crystals or rounds in main color (MC)
- 100 leaves or small daggers
- 50 large daggers
- 50 drops
- 50 4mm fire-polished crystals in contrasting color (CC)
- 2 focal beads and one small bead for each to use as a stopper (optional)
- C-Lon Bead Cord

MAKE IT!
String 8 main color (MC). Then string *[4 large daggers, 4 leaves or small daggers, 4 drops, 4 leaves or small daggers, 4 large daggers, 4 MC]; repeat from * 5 more times.

String 24 CC.

Set aside 32 MC and string the remainder of the MC beads.

63

String 24 CC.

String 4 MC. Then string *[4 large daggers, 4 leaves or small daggers, 4 drops, 4 leaves or small daggers, 4 MC]; repeat from * 5 more times.

End by stringing 8 MC.

Work in circular crochet four beads around until lariat is complete. End off your thread. Finish off as for Open End Without or with Focal Beads (page 48).

NEXT TIME . . .

Work smaller! Substitute 4mm beads with size 8/0 seed beads and use small daggers, drops, and leaves.

◎◎ MA VIE EN COULEUR ◎◎

BY BERT

Just look around you! They say nature is never wrong, and how right they are. In the 1960s, green and blue were all the rage for clothing and home furnishings. When you think about the fact that the sky is blue and the grass is green, you understand why this combination really works. But I like to stray from what's comfortable and challenge myself to see things differently. For example, I would add a touch of red to this blue-green mix (red like clay earth, to stay with the nature comparison). For me, this is the extra "hit" that creates dimension and interest.

This is how I approach most of my work. I begin by choosing a few colors inspired by nature or the world around me that are subtly varied or even monochromatic, and then add something unexpected.

If your first instinct is visually pleasing to you, don't let anyone else influence your choices; if you are disappointed, make a change! Often when inspiration strikes, I'm sure that what I've envisioned is perfect; then I string a section, crochet a sample, and realize that the combination doesn't work at all. Sometimes all it takes is for me to change one color and suddenly it all comes together.

The moral of this story is twofold: first, experiment with small swatch sections to spare yourself the heartache of having to restart a project after stringing an entire piece. Second, don't be discouraged if your initial choices aren't the best ones; replace one element at a time and eventually a visceral reaction will let you know when your color combination is harmonious.

II. CONVERTIBLE BROOCH/NECKLACE

DESIGNED BY BERT AND DANA

Everyone likes to get multiple uses from one object. We designed this piece with such versatility in mind. It can be worn either as a brooch or as the centerpiece of a necklace, since the "pendant" is detachable. Make several different necklace ropes—some long, some short, some casual, and others formal—so you can change the look of the centerpiece according to your mood.

WHAT YOU NEED

FOR PENDANT:

- 30 daggers in color A
- 30 daggers in color B
- 30 long drops
- 30 leaves
- 10 6/0 seed beads "bead soup" in main color (MC) (see Soup-er Versatile Necklace page 57)
- C-Lon Bead Cord
- 2 soldered jump rings
- 1 safety pin–shaped brooch finding (with **no** coil, or with a coil small enough for the jump rings to slip over)

FOR NECKLACE ROPE

- 2 tubes 6/0 seed bead "bead soup" (mix) in main color (MC)
- 36 6/0 seed beads in contrasting color (CC)
- C-Lon Bead Cord
- 2 spring rings or lobster claw clasps

MAKE IT!

PENDANT: String 5 MC. Then string *[3 A, 1 leaf, 3 B, 1 leaf, 3 drops, 1 leaf]; repeat from * 9 more times. Then string 5 MC.

Work in circular crochet five around until you have crocheted all your beads. Attach a jump ring to each end of the piece using the same method as for finishing an "Open End with a Clasp or Button" on page 49. (**NOTE:** You will not have a bail on the jump ring, so just sew into the ring itself.)

NECKLACE ROPE: String 18 MC and 13 CC. Then string all but 18 MC.

String on 13 CC and remaining 18 MC.

Work in circular crochet three around until you have crocheted all your beads. End off your thread.

Attach a spring ring or lobster claw clasp to each end of the rope

TO WEAR AS A BROOCH: Slide both jump rings of pendant onto the pin so that they sit on the closed side of the brooch.

TO WEAR AS A NECKLACE: Attach one clasp to each jump ring

NEXT TIME . . .

Experiment with different necklace and pendant lengths.

III. BRACELET

DESIGNED BY DANA

Inspired by Polynesian and Hawaiian leis, this bracelet uses a variety of floral elements. Living flowers become something entirely new when they are strung together to make a piece of jewelry. Similarly, beads shaped like flowers and leaves can be used in unusual ways to create designs that do not always have a floral appearance. Although this bracelet has an organic appearance, the beads are not immediately recognizable as leaves.

WHAT YOU NEED
- 40 8mm fire-polished crystals
- 88 leaves in main color (MC)
- 44 leaves in contrasting color (CC)
- C-Lon Bead Cord
- Toggle or clasp

MAKE IT!
String 4 leaves in MC. Then string *[4 leaves in CC, 4 leaves in MC, 4 fire-polished crystals]; repeat from * 9 more times. End by stringing 4 leaves in MC, 4 leaves in CC, 4 leaves in MC.

Work in circular crochet four beads around until you have crocheted all your beads. End off your thread

Finish with a toggle or clasp. (Open End with Clasp page 49).

NEXT TIME . . .
Try using many colors of leaves and string 12 of them randomly between the fire-polished crystal sections.

THE MARY NECKLACE

DESIGNED BY BERT

Mary and her daughter Meaghan began studying with us in September 2007. Their goal was to make jewelry they could sell to raise money for their nonprofit organization, The Freshman Fifteen. The Freshman Fifteen assists select college-bound students by providing them with dorm-room essentials. Mary and Meaghan have dedicated endless hours to producing beautiful work, all of which they sell to give 100 percent of the profits to their cause. When their inventory first became saturated, we insisted that Mary make something for herself. I designed this versatile piece that can be worn long or doubled, day into night.

WHAT YOU NEED

- 725 4mm fire-polished crystals in color A
- 725 4mm fire-polished crystals in color B (should be similar to color A)
- 164 drops
- 2 10mm flat rondelles
- C-Lon Bead Cord

MAKE IT!

String *[6 A, 1 drop, 6 B, 1 drop]; repeat from * 81 more times.

Then string *[6 A, 6 B]; repeat from * 11 more times (this section will become the toggle loop).

Work in circular crochet four beads around. Set aside.

TO MAKE TOGGLE BAR: String *[6 A, 6 B]; repeat from * 6 more times.

Work in circular crochet 4 beads around.

Follow STEP 1 of "Finishing Circular Crochet Projects" (page 47), and bury the ending tail.

String one flat rondelle and one 4mm bead

onto the starting tail. Sew the tail back through the rondelle, and all the way down through the toggle bar until it comes out of the ending side. String on the other rondelle and another 4mm bead. Sew back down into the toggle bar and through the first rondelle and first 4mm bead. Reinforce by going back down through the first rondelle, the toggle bar, and the second rondelle and 4mm. Come back through the second rondelle into your toggle bar, making sure that your rondelles and 4mm end beads are all taut (there shouldn't be any slack). Bury your thread.

FINISHING: Make a toggle loop using the section of rope that does not contain drops (see finishing instructions for "Toggle Loop" on page 50).

TO ATTACH THE TOGGLE BAR: Using the beginning tail of the rope, pick up three 4mm beads and sew straight through the middle of the toggle bar. Push the toggle bar and 4mm beads right up against the rope. Sew back down into the toggle bar. 4 mm beads and into the necklace rope. Reinforce this join several times by sewing back into the toggle bar, the 4mm beads, the toggle bar again, and the rope. Bury your tail neatly in the necklace.

NEXT TIME . . .
Substitute small leaves or another shape for the drops.

◉◉ NO GOOD DEED GOES UNREWARDED ◉◉

Mary had been interested in learning bead crochet for several years, but had nearly given up hope; her former attempts of finding private lessons for this purpose had been in vain. In September 2007, shortly after we began teaching, Mary was searching the Internet at 2 A.M. and stumbled across our Web site. At the same time, we had been looking for a charity with which to become affiliated. We knew we wanted to support a cause that benefited young people and possibly involved education, but we couldn't find one that was the right fit. We

 were as excited to find The Freshman Fifteen as Mary was to find teachers. It was kismet.

After her first lesson, Mary wondered if her daughter Meaghan would be interested in learning the technique, even though she had

never shown an interest in crafting before. Meaghan joined Mary at the second lesson, and we were all shocked and delighted to discover she was a prodigy. At this early stage, none of us could have guessed how our relationship would evolve over the years.

As The Freshman Fifteen grew, thanks to the successful sales of the magnificent jewelry Mary and Meaghan were producing, so did our friendship. We have learned so much about one another and ourselves through our lessons, and have become as close as family. We look forward to the continued growth and success of The Freshman Fifteen, and hope that countless students will ultimately benefit from the amazing work that Mary and Meaghan have done and continue to do. Learn more at www.thefreshmanfifteen.org.

TUTTI-FRUTTI NECKLACE

DESIGNED BY DANA

When I was growing up, my best friend had a pair of vintage cherry earrings that I coveted. Two Bakelite cherries dangled from each of her ears and made a "clicking" sound when they knocked together, every time she turned her head. Years later, I'm still mesmerized by this sound. I designed this necklace eagerly trying to recapture the playfulness of those earrings.

My mom, in turn, was inspired by my design and sought to incorporate some of her own favorite aesthetic, using African beads and a subdued palette. Her ethnic interpretation reminds us that we all see the world a little differently, and that's a beautiful thing.

WHAT YOU NEED

- 16 charms—you can either make your own, as I did, or use existing ones. If you choose to make your own, you will need several large beads of your choice. I designed four different charms and made four of each type.
- 16 headpins (if you are making charms)
- Round-nose pliers (if you are making charms)
- Wire cutters (if you are making charms)
- Less than 1 tube of 8/0 seed beads in color A (A)
- Less than 1 tube of 8/0 seed beads in color B (B)
- 1–2 tubes of 6/0 seed beads in main color (MC)
- Less than 1 tube of 6/0 seed beads in color C (C)
- Less than 1 tube of 6/0 seed beads in color D (D)
- 1 large button with 4 holes
- C-Lon Bead Cord

MAKE IT!

CHARM (make 16): Put the desired bead(s) onto a headpin [1]. Bend the headpin 90 degrees and cut it to about ¼ inch [2]. Hold the pliers in your hand so that your palm is facing you and grab the end of the

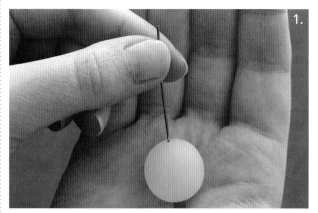

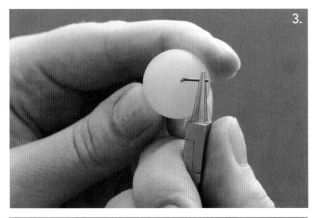

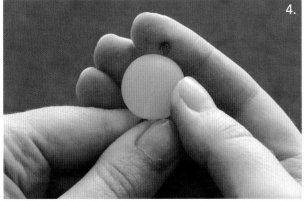

headpin [3]. Roll your wrist toward the bead, forming a closed loop [4].

NOTE: Although the images show a single bead, the method is the same for any number of beads you have on your charm.

PENDANT: String 120 A. Then string *[8 A, 4 C, 1 charm, 1 C, 1 charm, 2 C, 1 charm, 1 C, 1 charm, 4 C]; repeat from * 3 more times.

Note: If your charms are different, you may want to use one of each in a section and string them in the same order every round. This way, the charms will be evenly distributed around the pendant.

Work in circular crochet four beads around until you have worked all your beads. Crochet the charms as though they were beads, being careful not to skip those stitches on the following round. The long section of solid A will be the bail of the pendant. When you finish crocheting, leave the piece on a safety pin and do not cut the thread. You may need to add or remove some beads to make it fit properly around your rope.

ROPE: String 200 B and 12 C. Then string *[10 MC, 1 C, 10 MC, 1 C, 10 MC, 1 D, 10 MC, 1 D]; repeat from * until you have strung four times the desired length of your necklace. (The piece shown was approximately 100 inches, strung for a 25-inch necklace.)

Leave a 12-inch tail. Work in circular crochet four beads around until you get to B.

At this point, decrease to three around in the following manner: Insert your hook into the next stitch as normal and make a stitch without a bead. Continue as normal, and skip the empty stitch on the next round.

When you finish crocheting, do not cut your thread. This section of B will be the button loop, so you may need to add or remove some beads.

FINISHING: Make sure the bail of the pendant fits comfortably around your rope. It should be snug enough that it doesn't move around but loose enough that it can slide into a different position if you so desire. Remove any unnecessary beads, or add more from the back and crochet until you have established the correct length. Finish off as for a Toggle Loop(page 50).

ATTACH BUTTON: Thread your starting tail onto a needle and reposition your thread so that you are coming out of the side of the rope, close to the top. Pick up 4 MC, go up through one buttonhole (from back to front), pick up [1 MC, 2 8/0 seed beads in a contrasting color (these may be beads that you used

in your piece or a new accent color), 1 MC], go into the diagonal buttonhole from front to back, pick up 4 MC. Sew tightly into the rope and come back out next to the two sets of MC that you just added. Pick up 4 MC, go up into one of the two empty buttonholes, pick up [1 MC, 3 8/0 seed beads, 1 MC], cross over the existing beads and down into the remaining empty hole, pick up 4 MC and sew into the rope. Bury your tail.

BUTTON (OR TOGGLE) LOOP: Make sure your loop is the appropriate size for your button. It should be snug but loose enough for you to be able to open and close the necklace. Remove or add beads as necessary. End off your thread. Finish off as for a Toggle Loop (page 50).

NEXT TIME . . .
Use crystal charms and beads for a super-bling version.

INTERMEDIATE
CIRCULAR CROCHET PROJECTS

All of the projects in this section require invisible join closures,

a process described in the following section.

HOW TO CLOSE CIRCULAR CROCHET PROJECT WITH AN INVISIBLE JOIN

THE GREEN BEAD IS THE HIGH BEAD

THE YELLOW BEAD IS THE HIGH BEAD

The easiest way to learn this tricky join is with a four-, five-, or six-color spiral piece using a single size bead (such as Companion Bangles, on page 85).

1. Hold your piece so that the side where you started is on your right and the side where you finished is on your left.

Locate the highest bead on the ending side. It is the last bead you crocheted, and also the one next to the knot.

2. Locate the high bead on the starting side. It is the first bead you crocheted.

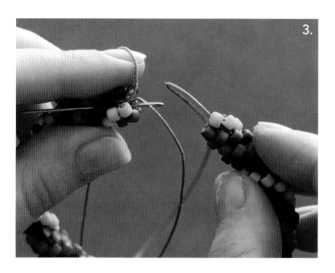

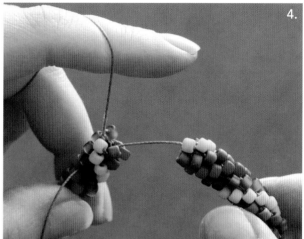

MAKE SURE YOUR SPIRALS LINE UP!

3. Thread a darning needle onto the beginning tail and sew into the center of the ending side, coming out about ¼ inch into the piece.

4. Pull this tail to bring the two ends together.

5. Remove the darning needle and thread it onto the ending tail. Fit the two sides together by matching the first and last beads you crocheted. Because they are both high beads, they interlock. Make sure that your spirals line up; if they don't, your piece will not close properly or neatly.

NOTE: If your spirals do not line up, check that you have crocheted all the beads in the pattern sequence. For example, in a four-color spiral pattern the first bead you crochet is color D, so the last bead you crochet has to be color A. If your spirals don't match up, pull out a few beads from the last row until you have ended with the correct bead in the sequence.

6.

THE NEEDLE SHOULD BE POINTING TOWARD YOU

7.

8.

KEEP ROLLING THE PIECE SO YOU CAN SEE THE PART WHERE YOU ARE WORKING

8. Repeat these two steps all the way around, remembering to alternate going into a bead on the right and going into a bead on the left. Also, remember that your needle is always coming toward you. You can rotate the piece a little bit, so that the two beads you are joining are always in your view.

NOTE: you never sew into a bead, only into a thread loop.

6. Insert your needle into the first thread loop on the beginning (right) side from behind the piece, so that it is coming out pointing toward you, and pull through.

7. Now insert your needle into the next thread loop on the ending (left) side, in the same way you would your hook (with the bead to the right) and pull through toward you. You will be inserting your needle from right to left, or from closer to the join to farther away from the join. Pulling the thread toward you will reorient the bead and bring it into place.

82

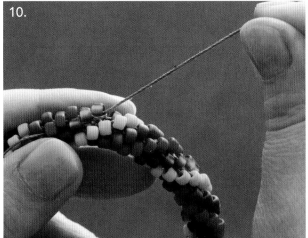

- If you are working with a pattern, make sure you crochet until the end of the sequence before you finish off your thread.

- If you are working with a solid color or a soup, you still need to finish your work in the right place. Before you finish crocheting, bring the two ends of your piece together and see if they "lock" correctly. If you have to twist the two ends to fit together properly, you will need to add or pull out beads until they fit together without twisting.

- Before you bury your tails, make sure that your join looks nice and seamless. If it doesn't, take it out and start again. It's worth the effort, because it will mean the difference between your piece looking amateurish or professional.

9. The last bead you sew into will be on the left, and it will be the high bead on that side.

10. Bury the working thread into the right side of the piece, sewing it at least halfway around for a bracelet and at least 4 inches into a necklace. Bury the other thread into the left side in the same manner.

COMPANION BANGLES

DESIGNED BY DANA

One of my greatest concerns when traveling, second only to deciding which projects I'm going to work on while I'm away, is what jewelry to pack. After struggling with this problem for some time, I devised the perfect solution: simple monochromatic bangles that could be mixed and matched to coordinate with any outfit. Some days I wear one, other days up to five. I find that I wear these bangles most often even back home, because they are so easy to throw on with anything.

Because of their spiral design, the Companion Bangles are also the perfect project for learning the invisible join!

WHAT YOU NEED

- Size 8/0 or 6/0 seed beads in four, five, or six different shades of one color:
- If using 8/0 seed beads, approximately 100 beads of each color
- If using 6/0 seed beads, approximately 70 beads of each color
- C-Lon Bead Cord for the 6/0 seed beads
- C-Lon Bead Cord or C-Lon Fine Weight for the 8/0 seed beads

MAKE IT!

Arrange your beads in order from the lightest to the darkest shades. Label your beads A, B, C, D, etc., in order from lightest to darkest.

String *[1 A, 1 B, 1 C, 1 D (1 E, and 1 F, if desired)]; repeat from * until you have strung all your beads.

Work in circular crochet four, five, or six beads around. End off your thread.

Close with an Invisible Join (pages 80–83).

NEXT TIME . . .

Use 3mm or 4mm fire-polished crystals, so that you can add sparkle to any outfit.

◎◎ ON THE ROAD AGAIN— ◎◎
TRAVELING WITH BEADS

We love discovering new places and exploring the cultural intricacies of different regions, but some elements from home are essential to every trip we take. Critical to each travel experience is the continuation of the creative process.

One of the things we love so much about bead crochet is its portability. Once the beads are strung, you can work anywhere without the fear of lost materials. Before traveling, we always string as many projects as possible so that we can crochet them during our travels. As glad as we were to be bead crocheting, we struggled for years with the fact that there was no efficient way to string in transit or away from home, in case we wanted to design something new while we were on the move. We began talking about "how great it would be" to have an all-in-one system for transporting materials and working on projects. We wondered if such an accessory existed, and after a little research, discovered that indeed it did not.

In 2008 we began working with a manufacturer to help turn our idea into reality. We started by combining a work mat with a project bag that could be folded compactly for travel. We decided to make the project bag detachable, so that different projects could be kept in different bags that snapped into the work mat when so desired. The final feature was a clear pocket on the back of the work mat to hold instructions or photographs. Almost a year later, after countless prototypes, crises, and headaches, String-Me-Along and the compatible Project Exchange Bags were on the market.

The success of our product is due in no small part to the friends, colleagues, and students who have tested, shared, and promoted String-Me-Along, and who continue to do so. We hope you bring your beading with you wherever you go as we do, so that the moment inspiration strikes, you will be ready to create.

STRING-ME-ALONG

turn *choatic crafts*   INTO CONTAINED CREATIVITY

For our ad campaign (which includes an animated video of the character you see above),
we wanted to show people that we understood how it feels to be overwhelmed by
"craft chaos." String-Me-Along helps solve that problem for us, and we hope that
it will for countless others! To learn more, visit our Web site:
www.welldoneexperience.com/shop.

VARIEGATED NECKLACE

DESIGNED BY BERT

We all sometimes find ourselves in a position of wanting to create something but are unable to decide what to make. At these times, I look at items I really love and reinterpret them into beadwork. A version of this necklace, for example, was inspired by my favorite scarf. Dana loved this idea, and chose one of her scarves to use as a point of departure to design her own version of this piece (as seen on page 101).

Choosing one overall color palette with a few contrasting colors makes this necklace exceptional. Try arranging your beads in a subtle gradation and throw in a couple of unexpected accents.

WHAT YOU NEED

- 13 colors of 4mm fire-polished crystals in the following quantities: Color A: 132; B: 68; C: 180; D: 92; E: 32; F: 124; G: 56; H: 92; I: 28; J: 60; K: 48; L: 68; M: 24
- C-Lon Bead Cord

NOTE: Colors E and F are the contrasting colors.

MAKE IT!

SHORT VERSION: String *[88 A, 44 B, 120 C, 60 D, 12 E, 80 F, 36 G, 52 H, 20 I, 40 J, 32 K, 56 L, 24 M, 12 L, 16 K, 20 J, 8 I, 20 E, 44 A, 24 B, 60 C, 32 D, 40 H, 20 G, 44 F] once.

LONG VERSION: Repeat from * one more time.

Work in circular crochet four beads around. End off your thread.

Close with an Invisible Join (see pages 80–83).

NEXT TIME . . .

Use 6/0 seed beads instead of fire-polished crystals for a more casual final product.

THE DANA BANGLE

DESIGNED BY DANA

Necessity is the mother of invention.

When I designed this bangle, I had no idea what a success this simple project was going to be. I had a few leftover 4mm beads in a color that I loved—but there weren't quite enough to make a complete bracelet. Out of necessity, I added the 6mm beads, and the Dana Bangle was born. Since then, I have barely been able to produce these bracelets fast enough to meet the constant demand for them. These bangles look best when two or three are worn together.

WHAT YOU NEED

- 56 6mm fire-polished crystals
- 156 4mm fire-polished crystals
- C-Lon Bead Cord

MAKE IT!

String on the 6mm crystals. Then string on the 4mm crystals.

Work in circular crochet four beads around. End off your thread

Close with an Invisible Join (see pages 80–83).

NEXT TIME . . .

Try making two bangles with inverse colors for a complementary look. For example, black 4mm with white 6mm crystals, and white 4mm with black 6mm crystals.

THE DANA BANGLE: TAKE TWO

DESIGNED BY DANA

After years of success selling the original Dana Bangle, I knew that I needed another simple bracelet to add to the line. This one looks great on its own or when paired with the original. The easy pattern is a fascinating combination of a stripe, a spiral, and a dot.

WHAT YOU NEED

- 70 4mm fire-polished crystals in color A
- 70 4mm fire-polished crystals in color B
- 70 6mm fire-polished crystals in color C
- C-Lon Bead Cord

MAKE IT!

String *[1 A, 1 B, 1 C]; repeat from * until you have strung all your beads.

Work in circular crochet four beads around. End off your thread.

Close with an Invisible Join (see pages 80–83), making sure to twist the rope slightly so that the pattern subtly spirals.

NEXT TIME . . .

Make a chunkier version by using two colors of 6mm crystals and one color of 8mm crystals.

GIVE ME A RING NECKLACE

DESIGNED BY DANA

I have always loved the way circular objects fit neatly into one another but can move independently, as they do in a gyroscope. This design is a modern interpretation of that idea: Two circles usually nest, but occasionally they move separately.

WHAT YOU NEED

- 600 4mm fire-polished crystals in color A
- 600 4mm fire-polished crystals in color B
- (Note: Colors A and B should be similar—they will be blended together in a soup to make the main color [MC].)
- 300 4mm fire-polished crystals in a contrasting color (CC)
- C-Lon Bead Cord

MAKE IT!

NECKLACE: Mix the 4mm fire-polished crystals in colors A and B to make a soup. String all 1,200 beads.

Work in circular crochet four beads around and end off your thread.

SMALLER RING: String on 120 CC. Work in circular crochet four around until your ring fits comfortably around the rope. End off your thread. Close with an Invisible Join (see pages 80–83).

LARGER RING: String on 180 CC. Work in circular crochet four around until this ring fits comfortably around the smaller ring. Note that the two rings should nest snugly. End off your thread. Close with an Invisible Join (see pages 80–83).

String the two rings onto your necklace and make sure one fits into the other properly. Close necklace with an Invisible Join (see pages 80–83) Tie an overhand knot that sits just above the two rings, securing them in place.

NEXT TIME . . .

Use 8/0 seed beads for the rope, for a lighter, more casual look. The rope shown at left was strung in the simple pattern: 6 MC, 1 CC, repeat. Crochet four around.

PUZZLE BRACELET

DESIGNED BY BERT AND DANA

Inspired by Cartier's Trinity rings, this bracelet is an elegant addition to any outfit. Use metallic beads to make a more traditional version, or use seed beads for a contemporary interpretation. The simple patterning adds extra texture.

WHAT YOU NEED

- About 1 tube each size 8/0 seed beads in colors A, B, and C
- (Less than) 1 tube size 8/0 seed beads in color D
- C-Lon Bead Cord

MAKE IT!

FIRST BANGLE: String *[2 A, 1 D]; repeat from * until you have strung most of the A beads. Work in circular crochet five beads around, until your piece is 1½ inches longer than your desired bracelet length. End off your thread.

SECOND BANGLE: String *[2 B, 1 D]; repeat from * until you have strung most of the B beads. Work in circular crochet five beads around, until your piece is the same length as the first bangle. End off your thread.

THIRD BANGLE: String *[2 C, 1 D]; repeat from * until you have strung most of the C beads. Work in circular crochet five beads around, until your piece is the same length as the first and second bangles. End off your thread.

ASSEMBLY: Close the first bangle with an Invisible Join (see pages 80–83).

Insert the second bangle through the opening of the first and close with an Invisible Join (see pages 80–83), so that the two are linked.

Insert the third bangle through the openings of both the first and second bangles and close with an Invisible Join, so that it is linked around both.

NEXT TIME . . .

Make only two bangles, the first strung 2 A, 1 B and the second strung 2 B, 1 A. Close as for the first and second bangles.

LINKED-TOGETHER NECKLACE

DESIGNED BY BERT

I love items and artwork that are out of scale, which is why for many years I was an obsessed dollhouse builder. In this case, I decided to enlarge a traditional chain and create a chunky, colorful necklace. I especially like the juxtaposition of each large ring being made with small beads. The shading created by subtle changes in color enhances the three-dimensional nature of the piece.

WHAT YOU NEED

- 1,000 6/0 seed beads in color A
- 500 6/0 seed beads in a contrasting color to color A (AA)
- 200 6/0 seed beads in color B
- 100 6/0 seed beads in a contrasting color to color B (BB)
- 200 6/0 seed beads in color C
- 100 6/0 seed beads in a contrasting color to color C (CC)
- C-Lon Bead Cord

MAKE IT!

CENTER LINK (make one): String *[2 A, 1 AA]; repeat from * 63 more times. Work in circular crochet four around until you have crocheted all your beads. This strip and the following should measure approximately 7 inches. End off your thread.

ADJACENT LINK 1 (make two): String *[2 B, 1 BB]; repeat from * 63 more times. Work in circular crochet four around until you have worked all your beads. End off your thread.

ADJACENT LINK 2 (make two): String *[2 C, 1 CC]; repeat from * 63 more times. Work in circular crochet four around until you have crocheted all your beads. End off your thread.

ROPE: String *[2 A, 1 B]; repeat from * until you have strung all your beads. Work in circular crochet four around until you have crocheted all your beads. End off your thread.

ASSEMBLY: Close the center link with an invisible join.

Thread an adjacent link 1 through this ring and close with an Invisible Join (see pages 80–83).

Repeat with the other adjacent link.

Thread an adjacent link 2 through one adjacent link 1. Close with an Invisible Join 1.

Thread the other adjacent link 2 through the other adjacent link 1. Close with an Invisible Join.

Attach one end of the rope to either adjacent link 2, using the same method for creating a Toggle Loop (see page 50). Attach the other end of the rope to the other adjacent link 2 using the same method.

NEXT TIME . . .

Make five different-colored links to create a rainbow effect.

◎◎ INSPIRATION IS EVERYWHERE ◎◎

Organization is one key to unearthing inspiration. When we find ourselves with "designer's block," we rearrange some of our supplies to stay productive and avoid inertia. Inevitably during this process of organizing our yarn, beads, buttons, fabrics, etc., two items we would never normally use in combination end up next to each other and look amazing. Often, while striving for order we must first make chaos.

It is essential never to stop the search for inspiration. Look through magazines and books regularly, notice what images you are attracted to, and analyze why. Is it the colors, shapes, composition, or all three? Just because you're making jewelry doesn't mean that you should be inspired only by accessories. Look at images of nature, animals, and art. Advertisements are an incredible source of inspiration, because their design fundamentals also apply to jewelry making. The color combinations, composition, texture, and thematic devices that make advertisements appealing are the same as for jewelry. Tear out or photocopy the images that attract you, and collect them in a book.

Carry a camera with you; buy postcards or wrapping paper with the images that interest you; save packaging from food and toys. There is no "right" or "wrong" when it comes to inspiration; it's a personal feeling that only you can harness. Just remember to keep your eyes open!

THESE ARE THE SCARVES THAT INSPIRED OUR COLOR CHOICES FOR THE ORIGINAL VARIEGATED NECKLACES

TWISTED NECKLACE

DESIGNED BY BERT AND DANA

We have both worked with yarn for many years, in retail and as avid knitters and crocheters. When unrolled skeins of yarn become loose, it is necessary to put them back into the neat little bundle that looks like a pastry twist. To do so, insert your hands into the center of an open skein, and pull the ends away from each other so that the skein is taut. Twist each of your hands in opposite directions; when you bring them together, the skein twists neatly back on itself. One end is tucked into the other, and the bundle looks like new.

It was this funny little method of handling yarn that inspired the design for this necklace. By twisting the ends in opposite directions, the two sides of the necklace neatly (and permanently) intertwine.

WHAT YOU NEED

- 900 pinch beads in color A
- 1,200 4mm round or fire-polished beads in color B
- 250 size 6/0 seed beads in color C
- C-Lon Bead Cord

MAKE IT!

ROPE 1: String all your pinch beads. Work in circular crochet four around, until you have crocheted all your beads. End off your thread.

ROPE 2: String all your fire-polished beads. Work in circular crochet four around until you have crocheted all your beads. End off your thread.

Make sure that your two ropes are of equal length. If they differ, shorten the longer rope so that the two ropes are the same length.

ACCENT RING (make two): String all your seed beads. Work in circular crochet four around and

make a rope that is approximately 3½ inches long. End off your thread.

ASSEMBLY: Connect one end of each of the two long ropes with an invisible join. Hold one end of your now-continuous rope in each hand. Twist one end clockwise and the other end counterclockwise (one away from you and one toward you). As you do this, slowly bring your hands closer together. Your necklace will begin to twist. The more you twist, the shorter your necklace will become, so make sure your piece will still fit over your head. When your piece has as many twists as you like, insert one end through the loop made by the first join. Then connect the two open ends with an Invisible Join

(pages 80–83), forming a link. Adjust your joins so that each link is a solid color.

Wrap one accent ring around the base of one linking end, so that it covers the invisible join. It should fit snugly enough that it won't slide, but not so tightly that its two ends won't meet comfortably. Close with an Invisible Join. Repeat with the other accent ring on the other linking end.

NEXT TIME . . .
Use three shades of the same color, with the brightest one used for the short ropes.

◎◎ MY MOM IS MY INSPIRATION ◎◎

BY DANA

Nothing ever stops my mom, a fact that never ceases to amaze and inspire me. In January 2007, just as we were launching our company, The Well Done Experience, my mom was afflicted with Bell's palsy. The right side of her face was completely paralyzed; her right eye

couldn't shut, requiring the use of an eye patch, and she was nearly unrecognizable. Though I could intellectually acknowledge what was happening, it was truly shocking to look at her face and see a woman I barely knew. We had no idea when the nerves in her face would begin to regenerate, if ever.

We both feared that in addition to potentially traumatic personal effects, the paralysis would be present at our first class, scheduled for the end of February. Would my mom be able to teach with an eye patch and slurred speech? Would she want to? Moreover, we worried the palsy would inhibit my mom's physical ability and desire to design and create beadwork.

Our fears were soon allayed; my mom (with her limited vision and the potential to become depressed, as so many paralysis victims do) refused to stop beading. She used the pony beads and yarn that we usually use for demonstration to create two beautiful, giant bead crochet lariats. My mom's determination and focus on creating art in her time of crisis proved invaluable; the nerves in her face soon began to "awaken," and not a trace of paralysis was left by the time we taught our first class. Every time I look at the lariats, which now hang in our office, I am reminded of the amazing ability crafting has to help us through our greatest challenges. More importantly, I am reminded of my mom's strength and determination, her powerful spirit that shines brighter than any star in the sky, and her unyielding belief that ultimately, everything always works out for the best.

FORGET-ME-KNOT BRACELET

DESIGNED BY DANA

I love the way traditional Chinese knotting looks and searched for a way to incorporate it into my beadwork. Since Chinese knotting requires thin cords (whereas bead crochet cords are thick), I had to find a way to adapt my inspiration. The result was a bracelet that does not technically include a knot but does create the illusion of one. By joining simple pieces together in this way, you can create a chunky bracelet that looks extremely elaborate.

WHAT YOU NEED

- 200 4mm fire-polished crystals in Color A
- 200 4mm fire-polished crystals in Color B
- One tube of 8/0 seed beads in color C
- C-Lon Bead Cord

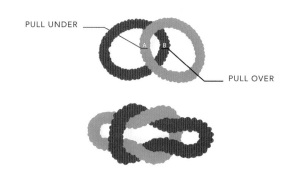

MAKE IT!

RING A: String all your 4mm crystals in color A. Work in circular crochet four around until all your beads have been crocheted. End off your thread. Close with Invisible Join (see pages 80–83).

RING B: String all your 4mm crystals in color B. Work in circular crochet four around until all your beads have been crocheted. End off your thread. Close with an Invisible Join.

BACK PIECES (make two): String half your seed beads. Crochet four around until you have a rope 10 inches long. End off your thread.

ASSEMBLY: Hold the A and B rings so that they overlap, with ring A on top. Reach into the B ring from beneath grabbing the A ring, and reach into the B ring from above grabbing the A ring, then pull.

Fold one seed-bead strip in half, forming a loop. Place the loop through one ring and bring the two ends through. Repeat with the second seed-bead strip.

Close one seed-bead strip with an Invisible Join. Bring the two ends of the other seed-bead strip through the newly created loop formed by the closure of the first seed-bead strip, and close with an Invisible Join.

NEXT TIME . . .

Make one seed-bead rope using thread to coordinate with ring A and the other seed-bead rope to coordinate with ring B. Attach each one to the opposite-colored ring.

ADVANCED
CIRCULAR CROCHET
PROJECTS

You now have all the technical knowledge you need to begin working with more difficult materials, such as tiny beads, thinner threads, and smaller crochet hooks. You might want to use cheater beads when beginning these projects—at least until you become more comfortable handling the materials (see "Advanced Tips and Tricks," page 125).

PLAITED BRACELET

DESIGNED BY DANA

I remember learning how to braid from my babysitter when I was a little girl. I loved the fact that she had worked with horses and used to braid their tails. As soon as I mastered the technique, every doll I owned with synthetic hair got this style. When I became a little older, I started focusing on my own hair. People were awed by the fact that I could French braid my own hair by the time I was 10 and often asked if they could watch me in the process.

My fascination with braids inspired this bracelet. By using three different colors, in addition to two different bead sizes, I was able to enhance the texture of the final product.

WHAT YOU NEED
- 300 3mm fire-polished crystals in color A
- 300 3mm fire-polished crystals in color B
- About ½ tube 11/0 seed beads
- C-Lon Fine Weight (for the 3mm beads)
- C-Lon Micro (for the 11/0 seed beads)

MAKE IT!
STRIP 1: String all your A beads. Work in circular crochet four around until your strip measures 9 inches. End off your thread.

STRIP 2: String all your B beads. Work in circular crochet four around until your strip measures 9 inches. End off your thread.

STRIP 3: String all your seed beads. Work in circular crochet six around until your strip measures 9 inches. End off your thread.

ASSEMBLY: Hold the three strips together in one hand. Use your dominant hand to braid the three strips together. The tighter your braid, the shorter your bracelet will be, so be sure to measure and adjust accordingly before closing. Join each piece with an Invisible Join (see pages 80–83), making sure you do not attach two different strips to each other. Before completing any single join, it is helpful to begin all three invisible joins by inserting the tail into the ending side to bring the pieces together.

NEXT TIME . . .
Make a chunkier version of this bracelet by substituting 8/0 seed beads for the 11/0 seed beads and 4mm fire polished crystals for the 3mm fire-polished crystals.

LUSTER-AND-CLUSTER NECKLACE

DESIGNED BY BERT

We love working with pearls and large stone chunks, but both of these materials are heavy if used to make a long necklace. By creating a piece with different sections, you can achieve the drama of using weighty materials while avoiding the discomfort of wearing a heavy final product. As always, we are fascinated by the interplay between sparkly crystals and organic materials. By combining these different elements, you can create both effect and comfort: The large chunks-and-pearl section is highlighted prominently by being worn in the front, while the lighter-weight, smoother crocheted rope rests around the back of the neck. A perfect balance of the aesthetic and the practical is achieved in this way.

WHAT YOU NEED

- 560 4mm fire-polished crystals in color A
- 72 4mm fire-polished beads in color B
- 160 5mm–6mm pearls
- 4 semiprecious large chunks (focal beads)
- 3 small focal beads (to be placed between the large chunks)
- C-Lon Bead Cord and C-Lon Fine Weight (or C-Lon Micro, depending on the size of the holes in the pearls)

MAKE IT!

Using C-Lon Fine Weight, string *[5 pearls, 1 A, 5 pearls, 1 B]; repeat from * 19 more times.

Work in circular crochet four around until you have crocheted all your beads. End off your thread.

Using C-Lon Bead Cord, string *[10 A, 1 B]; repeat from * 55 more times.

Work in circular crochet four around until you have crocheted all your beads. end off your thread

ASSEMBLY: Join the pearl section to the crystal rope using an Invisible Join (see pages 80–83). Attach the focal beads using the same method as finishing any project that is continous with focal beads. Be sure to reinforce with FireLine, as the beads are very heavy. (Semiprecious chunks often have sharp holes, so it is important to reinforce the join.)

NEXT TIME . . .

Use smoothly polished stone chunks with matte crystals to further push the interplay between "natural" versus "man-made."

◉◎ MY DAUGHTER IS MY INSPIRATION ◉◎

BY BERT

Dana is solid and earthy but feminine and angelic. Aside from lighting up my room when she enters, her choice of accessories and fashion is always surprising. She inspires the conservative side of me to take chances as she does; she makes choices I would never think to make and somehow manages to pull them off. She is strong yet delicate, refined

FASHIONISTA DANA AT 11 YEARS OLD

and offbeat—a balance that is evident in all aspects of her life, from her artwork to her interpersonal relationships.

She has taught me so much—not just through my observing her character but also because she shares her experiences with me. While she was a student at Barnard College she took a course in "Constraints and Creativity," a topic she discussed with me often. The central idea is that we can never be truly creative without limitations, and that often one's best work emerges from the most restrictive circumstance. When given only a few materials to work with, we can focus on the inner process as opposed to the external elements. Since then, I have tried to limit my choices when creating. Dana's knowledge and enthusiasm about this course have resonated in all areas of my life, not just in my artwork.

Most of all, Dana has taught me that we all see the world differently. Through raising her I discovered that everyone's creativity should be nurtured, respected, and appreciated. She and I may not always immediately agree on what design choices are best, but ultimately, through working together, we come to a conclusion that is stronger than any that either of us could have developed alone. We should all be encouraged to find our own creative voice, because by sharing and listening we can broaden one another's horizons.

DELICATE RING

DESIGNED BY BERT AND DANA

We often visit museums to admire jewelry that was made centuries ago. We are always awed by the craftsmanship and innovation displayed by the ancient Egyptians, Greeks, and Romans. These rings were inspired by a set of gold Byzantine bangles with jewels spaced evenly all the way around, displayed at the Metropolitan Museum of Art.

WHAT YOU NEED

- 136–168 2mm metal beads or semiprecious stones in main color (MC)
- 17–21 metal beads or semiprecious stones in contrasting color (CC)
- Optional: 1 accent bead or charm
- C-Lon Micro

NEXT TIME . . .
Use a 3mm contrasting bead for raised dots.

MAKE IT!

String *[8 MC, 1 CC]; repeat from * 17 to 21 times, depending on your ring size. If you are adding an accent bead or charm, string it on instead of a CC bead about halfway through.

Work in circular crochet four around until desired length. End off your thread.

NOTE: You must complete a sequence before finishing, or your two ends will not match up (e.g., end by crocheting 8 MC). Before you end off your thread, bring the two ends together to see if the piece will close nicely. Occasionally you will find that you have to twist the piece so much that the shape is compromised. In this case we recommend pulling out or adding a section.

Close with an Invisible Join (see pages 80–83).

RIBBON BROOCH

DESIGNED BY BERT AND DANA

We love the art of gift-wrapping. Over the years we have collected beautiful paper and ribbons that we use to make every presentation special. This delicate bow is reminiscent of that on a tiny present. We believe this diminutive treasure truly exemplifies the old adage "good things come in small packages."

WHAT YOU NEED
- 300 3mm fire-polished crystals in color A
- About ½ tube of 11/0 seed beads in color B
- 2 8mm beads in accent color
- Small pin-back finding
- C-Lon Fine Weight for 3mm crystals
- C-Lon Micro for 11/0 seed beads

MAKE IT!
String all A Crystals. Work in circular crochet four around until you have crocheted all of your crystals. Close with an Invisible Join (see pages 80–83).

String all the C beads. Work in circular crochet five around until you have a 9-inch rope. End off your thread. Finish both ends of the rope with an 8mm bead, as for a lariat (see Open End with Focal Bead page 48).

Make a slipknot with the seed-bead strip. Slip the A ring through the slipknot so that it is centered, and tighten the slipknot. Thread FireLine Braided Bead Thread onto a small needle and sew together the slipknot and the A cord. Using the same thread, sew a pin back to the back of the seed-bead strip vertically.

NEXT TIME . . .
Make a monochromatic version for a subtler outcome.

119

LINK EARRINGS

DESIGNED BY BERT AND DANA

The flexible nature of bead crochet makes this technique ideal for crafting rings to make links. It was difficult to decide at first how to attach these simple circles to an earring finding while maintaining movement. We forced ourselves to think outside of the box and come up with a creative solution to our assembly problem. This is just one of many times we needed to use trial and error to achieve a satisfactory final result. If your first idea of how to accomplish your design goal fails, don't give up! Often, when our imaginations are stretched, we reach the best results.

WHAT YOU NEED

- 240 2mm metal beads or semiprecious stones in color A
- 300 2mm metal beads or semiprecious stones in color B
- Toggle ring with a ¼-inch-diameter opening and a bail
- Earring wire or post
- C-Lon Micro (Note that in this project you will see a lot of thread, so decide whether you want it to be a contrasting or coordinating color.)

MAKE IT!

EARRING (make two): String 120 A.

Work in circular crochet three around until all your beads have been crocheted. End off your thread.

Slide the toggle ring onto this piece and close with an Invisible Join(see pages 80–83).

String 150 B.

Work in circular crochet three around until you have crocheted all your beads. End off your thread.

Link this piece with the A ring and close with an Invisible Join.

Attach an earring finding to the bail of the toggle ring.

NEXT TIME . . .

Make two small rings and one large ring for each earring, creating a longer piece and a more dramatic effect.

ADVANCED

TIPS AND TRICKS

A TRANSLUCENT YELLOW BEAD WITH THREE
DIFFERENT THREAD COLORS

AN OPAQUE PURPLE BEAD WITH THE SAME
THREE THREAD COLORS

MORE ABOUT THREAD CHOICE

As we have said, we do usually recommend using
the thickest thread the bead holes will allow.
Occasionally, however, you may wish to use a slightly
thinner thread; for example, you can use C-Lon Bead
Cord for size 8/0 seed beads, but in this case the
thread will be visible. If you prefer your thread to be
hidden, use C-Lon Fine Weight. The most important
thing is to be sure that the thread is strong enough
and that your piece is sufficiently flexible when
finished.

DESIGNING WITH THREAD

Many people believe that you should never show
your thread—that you should match thread to bead

TEAL THREAD WITH THREE DIFFERENT BEAD COLORS

color so it will ultimately "disappear" into the piece. We agree that at certain times, this is the best option; however, thread can be an exciting element in your beadwork, the component that turns your piece from ordinary to extraordinary.

If you're not sure what thread color to use, make small samples using several different colors. Sometimes you may want to match your thread color to your focal beads, which are a contrasting color to the rest of the beads in your piece

NAIL POLISH

If you are stringing your beads directly onto your thread without a needle, you can put a little dab of base-coat nail polish onto the end to stiffen it and prevent fraying. Keep in mind, however, that the added layer will make the thread thicker.

THE SAME BEAD SOUP WITH THREE DIFFERENT THREAD COLORS

HELP FROM PLIERS

You can use pliers to pull your needle and thread through a stubborn bead when you are stringing—but don't pull too hard; you may crack the bead!

You can also use pliers to pull the needle through when burying your tails.

KNOWING HOW MANY BEADS TO STRING

One easy way to approximate the number of beads you will need for a given project is to work up a small sample and multiply. For example, if 100 beads yield 1 inch of bead crocheted rope, then 700 beads will make 7-inch rope.

Another useful method for circular crochet is to wrap your strung beads around your wrist or neck the same number of times that you will be working beads around. In other words, if you are making a bracelet that is four around, wrap the strung beads around your hand four times (to be sure you have enough). Again, these are only approximations, so be sure to string a little bit more than you think you will need.

BRACELET LENGTH

There is no "standard wrist size." Depending on the thickness of the beaded bracelet, the final length will need to be adjusted. In other words, a 7½-inch length of beaded rope will have a different inner circumference when closed, depending on the thickness of the rope. For example, a bracelet made using 8/0 seed beads crocheted four around will have an larger inner circumference than one of the same length made using 6/0 seed beads crocheted four around.

When measuring for a bangle, especially when closing with an invisible join, the closed bangle should fit snugly around the widest part of your hand when you squeeze your hand together. If you measure around your wrist, you will not be able to push the bangle up past your hand.

If closing with focal beads, take into account how much length they will add to your bracelet. You will not need to crochet as much as you would if you were closing with an invisible join.

When measuring for a bracelet that will be closed with a clasp, you can measure around your wrist.

CHEATER BEADS

Starting circular crochet can be difficult—especially when using one color, small beads, or shapes. There is a simple trick to help you get started. First, string all the beads for your project, then string on a few rows of either 6/0 or 4mm beads. If your difficulty comes from crocheting a single color, you can string the cheater beads in a four-color (spiral) pattern. If the problem is simply that your beads are too small

to begin your rope comfortably, you can use a few rows of a solid color.

At the end, pull out the cheater beads one at time from the back using a needle. Be especially careful not to go through the thread with your crochet hook when making your first stitches; if you do, you will not be able to pull out the cheater beads easily.

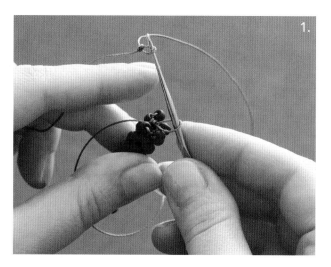

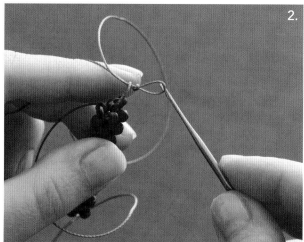

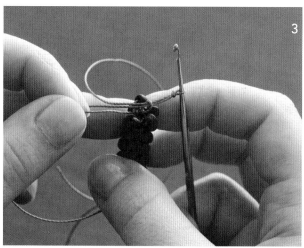

ADDING THREAD TO CIRCULAR CROCHET PIECES

If you have a severe stringing mistake that cannot be solved by killing beads (see page 128), or if you have crocheted all of your beads and realize your piece isn't long enough, you have the option of adding thread.

1. Leave the working loop of your thread open and cut the end of your thread, leaving an 8-inch tail. String all of your beads onto the new thread you wish to join. Make a slipknot at the end of the new thread, leaving an 8-inch tail. Insert your hook into the working loop (from the piece you were crocheting) and grab the new slipknot with your hook.

2. Pull the new slipknot through the working loop, making sure that the knot comes through as well (so that it is on the inside of the rope).

3. Pull the old tail to tighten into place.

4. Begin working your piece using the new thread. When you have crocheted a full round, pull both tails to make sure they are fully tightened. Leave your two tails hanging out of the piece and bury them once you have completed your rope.

ADDING BEADS FROM THE BACK FOR CHAIN STITCH OR CIRCULAR CROCHET

5. In some cases it may not be necessary to add thread. If you need to lengthen your piece only a little bit, use this simple method: Unravel a long piece of your working thread from the spool and cut. Add the beads onto the end of the thread and continue crocheting as normal. If you have a pattern, remember to load the beads in reverse order (e.g., if you originally strung 1 A, 1 B, 1 C, you will have to string 1 C, 1 B, 1 A). Also remember that you use **much** more thread than you may think, especially for circular crochet; thread is your least expensive material, so it is better to waste some than to run out.

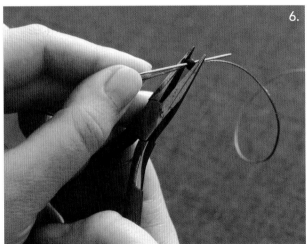

KILLING BEADS

6. If you come across a stringing mistake when you are well into your piece, don't panic! Identify the mistake and determine which beads need to be removed in order for your pattern to be corrected. Insert a needle into the bead to be killed and crack the bead using pliers. If you don't insert a needle, you risk tearing the thread. Shield your eyes and watch out for flying shards. You can also wrap the bead you are going to break in a cloth, which will keep the broken pieces contained.

ACKNOWLEDGMENTS

We are so grateful to everyone who has helped us on this journey: Joy Tutela, BJ Berti, Jasmine Faustino, George Ross, and Cathryn Schwing, for helping us make the dream of this book a reality; Maxine Levinson, Phyllis Howe, Karin Strom, and Ellie Joos, for guiding us on countless occasions; June Sung, Jonathan Swafford, Arturo Erbsman, Liza Garrin, and Patricia Fellman, for fulfilling all of our creative needs; Perry Bookstein, Anthony Nappi, Barry Kahn, Kim Rueth, Pearl Chin, and all our friends at York Novelty Import, Metalliferous, Caravan Beads, Knot Just Beads, and Knitty City; Marsha Davis, Christine Flanner, Arlene Mintzer, Etty Kattan, Mary Buckley, Meaghan Buckley, and all those who have inspired us to create beadwork over the years; Carl Unger, for always coming to our rescue; and to all of our friends and family, without whose unyielding support and love we never could have achieved our goals.

RESOURCES

Bead Biz
www.beadbiz.org

Bead My Love
www.beadmylove.com

Bead Q!
8584 East Washington St.
Chagrin Falls, OH 44023
(440) 708-1771
www.bead-q.com

Beads By Blanche
106 N. Washington Avenue
Bergenfield, NJ 07621
(201) 385-6225
beadsbyblanche.com

Boye Needle Company
www.simplicity.com/t-boye.aspx

Caravan Beads
915 Forest Avenue
Portland, ME 04103
(207) 761-2503 or
(800) 230-8941

Holy & Pure Gemstone, Inc.
(678) 482-8778
www.holygemstone.com

Knot Just Beads
4309 South 76th Street
Greenfield, WI 53220
(414) 771-8360
www.knotjustbeads.com

Metalliferous
34 West 46th Street
New York, NY 10036
(212) 944-0909
metalliferous.com

Ocean Dreams
48 West 48th Steet
New York, NY 10036
(212) 696-9247
www.oceandreamsusa.com

Susan Bates
www.coatsandclark.com

Shivam Imports
48 West 48th Street
New York, NY 10026
(212) 997-7512
http://shivamimportsny.com

Trinkets By T
www.trinketsbyt.com

Tulip Co., Ltd.
http://buy.caron.com

Unicorne Beads
(714) 572-8558
www.unicornebeads.com

York Novelty Imports Inc.
10 West 37th Street
New York, NY 10018
(212) 594-7074 or
(800) 223-6676
http://yorkbeads.com

ANNUAL BEAD SHOWS:

Bead and Button
(http://beadandbuttonshow.com)

Interweave Bead Fest
(www.beadfest.com/beadfest)

OUR WEBSITES:

www.chicken-egg.com

www.welldoneexperience.com

INDEX